I0457798

The Yankee And The British War Bride

The Memoirs of Ernest Joseph Donka and
Mary Irene Cooper-Dodd-Donka

GLASS**SPIDER**PUBLISHING

Copyright ©2025 Candace Carson

ISBN: 978-1-957917-86-3 (paperback)
ISBN: 978-1-957917-87-0 (e-book)

Library of Congress Control Number: 2025919042

All rights reserved. No part of this book may be reproduced, stored in a retrieval system, or transmitted in any form or by any means without prior written permission from the author, except for the use of brief quotations in a book review.

Visit the book website at www.donkafamilybook.com

Cover design by Judith S. Design & Creativity
www.judithsdesign.com
Published by Glass Spider Publishing
www.glassspiderpublishing.com

This book is dedicated to all the men and women around the world who served and fought in WWII. My wish is that their stories not be forgotten, and that we honor their bravery and their commitment to freedom for all.

Contents

Introduction

by Candace Carson

These are the handwritten memoirs of my mother, Mary Irene Cooper-Dodd-Donka of Tipton, Staffordshire, England, and my father, Ernest Joseph Donka of Aurora, Illinois. It is an account of their childhoods before World War II, their experiences during the war, and how they happened to meet and get married after the war in Aurora, Illinois on October 19, 1946.

In 1995, my father was diagnosed with multiple myeloma, a cancer that at the time had no cure. I had suggested journaling to my father as a way of passing the time and examining the emotions swirling through his mind as he faced the reality of life with cancer. He decided to write about his experiences of growing up during the Depression, as well as his time as a soldier in the Army during WWII.

Not wanting to be left out, my mother set out to write her own fascinating account of life as an adopted child who lived through the bombings in England, her service in the Signal Corps of the British Army, and her experiences with love and loss.

My mother's upbringing and her life before, during, and after the war will bring tears to your eyes. She describes her experiences during the late 1930s and the horrors of war as seen through the eyes of a child. She writes about her becoming a young adult serving her country in the British Armed Forces, and how she became a war bride to an American soldier—not my father.

Mary Irene Cooper was born on June 15, 1926, in County Durham, England, to Eleanor M. Cooper, a single nineteen-year-old girl who worked as a domestic servant in northern England. My mother had only one memory of her young childhood, as she writes at the beginning of her story. She had blocked out all earlier memories and experiences from her younger years—until a few days before her passing in June 2020.

She believed she entered the orphanage in Lichfield, England, around the age of two. However, we now know she was admitted to the Lichfield Orphanage on July 22, 1932, at the age of six, coming from the Durham Poor Law Institution. Although we don't know the exact date she was placed in the Durham Institution, we don't think she was there very long. It was her mother and stepfather who placed her in the Lichfield Orphanage on that July day.

In 2019, my niece Alex started researching Mom's history. Through DNA testing, we learned there was much more to Mom's life story than any of us had ever realized. Unfortunately, by the time we had the many details of her early life, Mom had developed dementia and was living with my sister, Cindy.

When we tried to tell her we'd found she had a half-sister living in Texas, she became very upset and angry with us. We decided for her mental health and well-being to never mention it again.

Through our research, we also discovered Mom not only had a half-sister named Joyce, but also a half-brother named George. All three children had different fathers.

The story below is told exactly as Mom remembered it. I have

7

not filled in all of the facts as we now know them to be. Mom actually had a much bigger family than she could ever have imagined. I will list her family and the true facts of her early life as best as I can at the end of her memoir.

Part I: Mary

Mary Irene Cooper-Dodd-Donka
Born June 15, 1926
Died June 21, 2020
Born in County Durham, England

My dearest Candy. So you want my life's story? I can tell you it will certainly be much different from your father's—and probably not as humorous—but I will try to make it interesting and maybe give you some insight into why I am the way I am.

When Daddy gets upset with me, he sometimes accuses me of thinking I am better than everyone else. In fact, the opposite is closer to the truth. I've always felt insecure and not quite as worthy as other people, so I'm always trying harder to please everyone. I can't stand arguments, or "rows" as we used to call them, but you will understand as my life unfolds before you. So here it goes.

Chapter 1: The Orphanage

My first clear memory of childhood is sitting on a stoop—a verandah, the kind that opens directly onto the sidewalk—with a young lady and a very pretty baby with blond curls. I was eating bread and treacle—a very sweet, very sticky treat, but oh, so good. I have no idea if this woman was a relative or maybe even my mother. I was told that my parents died in a car accident when I was a baby, but I have no idea if this is true or not. I could have been born to an unwed young girl for all I know.

My next vivid memory is living in an awful house with outdoor toilets and all kinds of children, from toddlers to bigger kids. Mostly what I remember about that time is that I was not happy. But I don't think my stay there was too long because I was still very young when I arrived at the orphanage in Litchfield (*Records show that she was six years old when she arrived at the orphanage, and that Elenor and Albert had released her into its care. Mom and Elenor may have spent a brief time at what was then called the "Poor House" before Elenor met Albert, or she may have been there for a short time before Elenor and Albert brought her to the Lichfield Orphanage*).

At the orphanage in Litchfield, there were two very large homes—one for boys and one for girls. Our house parents were

Mr. and Mrs. Campbell. What a difference from the first home I lived in! In my new home, I wore very pretty dresses and patent leather shoes. We had a building at the end of the play yard where we used to put on shows or plays, and we had such fun. Even before I was in school, I loved to sing and preform. They gave me a baby doll and I sang the song "Golden Slumbers." I later sang this same song to all my babies as I rocked them to sleep.

One spring, we were set to perform in the city, and I was supposed to be dressed like a toy soldier and sing, "There's something about a soldier, there's something about a soldier, there's something about a soldier, that's fine, fine, fine. For a military dress seems to suit the ladies best, there's something about a soldier that's fine, fine, fine." But lo and behold, on the day of the performance, I awoke with a case of the mumps.

Oh, how I cried as they tied up my chin with a scarf and told me I couldn't go to the performance. All I was allowed to do was watch the parade going out of the gates and down the lane. I was heartbroken.

In the front parlor of the girls' home was a very large radio. I remember thinking that someone must be inside that large box singing all those classical songs. I would listen to "Cornish Rhapsody," "The Blue Danube," compositions by Brahms, and many more wonderful songs. My love of music grew and grew.

I had a special friend named Marge Binfield who had a brother who lived on the boys' side of the orphanage. One day, Mrs. Campbell informed us that Marge and her brother were going home. I wasn't sure what "going home" meant—if they were being adopted or being sent back to their real parents. I don't remember if I cried, but things were never the same once my friend was gone. Life went on.

One day, I was swinging on the iron gates in front of the

orphanage when I got my little finger smashed in the gate. How that hurt! I still have the scar, and I vividly remember the horror of having it bandaged and soaked and re-bandaged daily until it healed.

We used to go to camps in the summer and sleep in tents. It was during one of those summers that I woke up and felt something in my ear. They took me the infirmary, where they removed a worm-like object from my ear. They called it an "earwig." I never heard of an earwig again until I was in the States living on Indian Avenue and our neighbor brought over a bug and asked, "Have you ever seen one of these?"

I knew right away what it was and told him it was an earwig. He laughed at me, but he went home and looked it up in an encyclopedia. Later, he came back to apologize and show me a picture of one.

About once a month, or so it seemed, we were all bathed and dressed in our best clothes. Visitors would come and look us over, and some of them would speak to us. Then, within a week or two, another friend would leave the orphanage. Matron would tell the rest of us that those children had been chosen to go home to live with new families.

As time went on, I grew saddened, wondering what was wrong with me. Why wasn't I chosen? I was very sweet, pretty, and well mannered. But Matron explained that most people wanted younger children. On Sundays we attended church at the Litchfield Cathedral, and the music would once again fill my soul and I forgot about being adopted for a while.

One Saturday, we went through the ritual again—getting bathed, having our hair washed and trimmed, and shoes shined— before we sat in the playroom waiting for our visitors. An older couple walked in. The lady was dressed in a shimmering blue dress, with a golden cross and chain resting on her chest, and a fur slung around her shoulder. I later learned it was a fox skin, head and tail and all! The man wore a dark blue suit. He had a mustache, curly iron-gray hair, and round-rimmed glasses. I thought he was the most handsome fellow I had ever seen, but the woman appeared a little stiff and stern.

A few weeks later, Matron came to me and said, "Mary, do you remember the man and woman who were here? Well, they have decided that they would like to take you home to live with them, and they are coming to get you next weekend."

I don't remember how I really felt when Matron explained that they wanted me because I was seven years old and they thought I was big enough to help with the housework. I just remember thinking, "But they're so old."

I really didn't mind too much. At the orphanage, I had been shown how to lay a proper table, shine shoes, and make beds. My only possessions were a stuffed orange fish and a small book. But the people who were taking me home said I didn't need to bring anything, just the clothes I was wearing, and that they would provide everything else I needed.

Chapter 2: Life with My New Parents

I clearly remember feeling very sad when Mrs. Campbell hugged me and told me to be a good girl. I was a little afraid, but soon I was enjoying my first train ride, sitting between these two strangers. It was quite a long walk from the train station to my new home. I was told to call them Mommy and Daddy, and that they would call me by my middle name, Irene. The reason was that they had lost a baby of their own named Mary.

When we got to their house, we had a light supper at the kitchen table, and I was shown which seat would be mine. That was where I sat for the rest of my years whenever we ate in the kitchen, which was mostly breakfast and supper in the late evening. Dinner at noon and tea at five were eaten in the sitting room.

I loved the sitting room, which had fine leather furniture. Even the top of the dining table was burgundy leather. The sitting room had a long sofa, a rocking chair, a huge armchair, a grandfather clock, an organ, a sewing machine, a radio, and a beautifully tiled fireplace.

There was a fireplace in each room, as we had no central

heating. The parlor was beautifully furnished with a flowered settee. At one end, the arm could be put down so that you could lie upon it. Of course no one ever did; the parlor was very seldom used. It also had a huge sideboard (dresser) with a mirror and three large round vases made of fine china with beautiful figures and flowers on them, encrusted with shiny stones. The best tea set, silverware, and linen tablecloths were kept in the sideboard. Huge paintings hung on the walls, and occasional chairs were placed around the room. It had a bay window with colored leaded windowpanes on top and a beautiful carved round table in front of it. I had never been in such a lovely house.

That first night, I slept on a cot that was placed alongside of their bed. My new mother had made me a beautiful, long white flannel nightgown trimmed with lace. She told me to kneel by the bed and say my prayers.

"Now I lay me down to sleep. I pray the Lord my soul to keep. If I should die before I wake, I pray the Lord my soul to take. And please God bless Mummy and Daddy and help me to be a good girl. Amen."

This became my nightly ritual, and to this very day I pray to God to help me be a better person.

After a few nights, after they learned I was not afraid of the dark or to sleep alone, I was given my very own bedroom. It had a big bed with a brass headboard and white porcelain decorations. I was also given a beautiful rose-pink comforter filled with down feathers. My room had gas lights and a gas heater in the fireplace, and a tall wardrobe with doors and drawers for all my clothes.

Mornings were wonderful. I would crawl into Mom and Dad's bed, and Daddy would bring us tea and biscuits (cookies). And so my new life began. They bought me new clothes and shoes. I was taken to the local school, St. Mark's, which was run by the

Episcopalian (Anglican) Church. Mr. Lockett was the headmaster. I didn't care for him at all, but the teachers seemed just fine.

One day, it was raining, and we couldn't go out to play. A group of boys were playing a game of marbles, and I needed to pass them. As I stepped around them, one of the boys lifted my skirt up, saying, "Let's see your knickers, Irene."

I kicked him in the pants and told him how cheeky he was. Then someone grabbed my arm roughly. "You had better come with me, young lady." It was the headmaster. He dragged me to his office, sat me down, scowled, and said, "We will not tolerate that kind of behavior. I am sending a letter home to your parents." He wouldn't let me explain what had happened.

When I went home and told Mummy and Daddy about it, Mummy agreed with me. "You were quite right, my girl. That boy had no business looking up your skirt, and don't you ever let anyone do that to you again."

I remember Mom and Dad wearing their best clothes, going to the school and demanding to see the boy who had done it. They made him apologize to me and said that if he ever touched me again, my dad would come and box his ears.

His name was Billy Harris. He was always laughing and joking. Ironically, we later became good friends, but I didn't dare tell my parents, as I knew they wouldn't approve. This same boy ran me over with his bike one rainy Sunday afternoon. I was running home from Sunday school, started to cross the road, and didn't see him. I still have the scar near my nose.

Getting hit by the bike didn't scare me half as much as the fact my lovely pale green Sunday-best coat was covered with blood and mud. Mummy took it to the cleaners, and because it didn't come back completely clean, she had them dye it navy blue. It became my school coat.

The only notable occasion while I was at St. Mark's was King George and Queen Mary's Silver Jubilee in 1935. It was a very grand day. The mayor of Tipton came to our school all dressed in his mayoral robes with a big gold chain and medallion. We sang patriotic songs and had tea and biscuits, and each child received a small mug with a picture of the king and queen on it to commemorate their jubilee. I still have it in the china cabinet, although the handle has come off. King George was Queen Elizabeth's grandfather.

On the first day of every May, we celebrated May Day and danced around a maypole decorated with long ribbons in bright colors. As we danced around the pole, we made a design that looked as if the ribbons had been braided around the pole. What fun we had. It was springtime, and I have always loved the springtime. The flowers began to bloom—snowdrops, daffodils, buttercups, daisies, and bluebells covered the forest floor. I used to pick the daisies and make daisy chains. Soon the lilacs would bloom, and Daddy would cut a huge armful for me to take into the house.

Mommy and Daddy's birthdays were also in May, the 14th and 16th. We always celebrated with a special tea: cucumber and salmon sandwiches, jelly and blancmange (Jell-O and custard), sponge cake with raspberry filling, and scones with butter and jam.

June came along, and with it the start of summer. The first Sunday of June was our Sunday school anniversary. We would have a parade around Gospel Oak where we lived and Ocker Hill, where most of the neighborhood children lived. I would have a new dress for the parade, and then another—a beautiful white silk dress with white silk hand-knit socks—for the afternoon and evening services.

I used to sing the solo parts along with another girl named

Barbra Cornfield. She was so beautiful. She had dark, curly hair and big brown eyes with long eyelashes, a peaches-and-cream complexion, and a lovely rosebud mouth. I envied her because she could dance—tap and ballet—and she would put on skits for the Sunday school children. We practiced our skits several nights a week for three or four weeks before the play, and then we charged a small admission to raise money for the missionaries. It was such fun.

The first Sunday in June also meant Daddy would harvest the first of the peas and tiny new potatoes, and we'd have roast leg of lamb. I used to help Mommy shell the peas and eat a few right out of the pod. Daddy had a wonderful vegetable garden behind the blacksmith shop, where he grew everything: peas, beans, carrots, parsnips, rutabagas, radishes, lettuce, cabbages. There were also bushes of blackberries, gooseberries, black currants, rhubarb, and elderberry trees.

I used to eat stalks of rhubarb with sugar, and Mom would make deep dish pies and cobblers with custard. When the berries and currants were ripe, I used to help Daddy pick them, and we always shared them with our neighbors. Sometimes, one or more of the neighbors would give me a sixpence.

Behind our house we had a flower garden, two apple trees, a lawn, and a pen where we raised chickens. The flower garden was tended to by Mommy. She had such beautiful roses, asters, daisies, snapdragons and wallflowers. In the back yard was the clothesline, and wash day was every Tuesday, come rain or shine. Wednesday was ironing day, done on the kitchen table with old folded blankets and sheets. The irons were called "sad irons" and heated on the kitchen hob. You had to keep two irons heating. When one got cold, you simply returned it to the grate and picked up the second one. Sheets, pillowcases, tablecloths, handkerchiefs, slips, dresses, shirts—everything was ironed.

After I turned eight or nine, I learned to iron, at first only small straight things like hankies, pillowcases, and napkins. I enjoyed doing this because it gave me great pleasure to see everything so neat and smooth. To this day, I still like to iron. (There was no electricity in my town until the year I first went back with Robin and David in the early 50s, at which time the city put it in every house. I bought my parents an electric iron and ironing board as a gift while I was home.)

When I was very young, Daddy built me a wooden swing at the very end of the garden. I used to swing on it for hours at a time because I could look over the neighbors' gardens and say hello to anyone who happened to be outside. Sometimes I would just swing and sing and make imaginary shapes and figures out of the clouds.

Sometimes I was allowed to cross the street and visit my dad at the smithy. He'd let me help pull the handle of the bellows, but I couldn't stay if there were any men there because, as Daddy said, "It was no place for a little girl." Oh, how I adored my dad!

When I was thirteen years old, I attended Tipton Central girls' school. It was a private school that you had to pass an entrance exam to get into, and as my parents didn't want me to go to a public school, that's where I went. We wore uniforms: white blouses and ties, navy blue jumpers, black stockings and shoes, and a black beret with our school badge on the front. In the summer, we wore blue-and-white cotton dresses with matching bloomers, which we had to make in sewing class. I took mine home and Mom helped me, as she was a wonderful dressmaker. We wore white anklets, white tennis shoes, and straw hats. I rode the bus to school if the weather was bad, but other times I rode my bike or walked, even though it was a very long walk.

My favorite class was English because our teacher, Miss Baker, was theatrical and made learning fun. One year, we read an American book called *Uncle Tom's Cabin*. It was about slavery in America, and we did a play about it. I was Topsy, a little Black girl with tiny braids.

And then, of course, we had sports, which I excelled in. Even though I was small, I was very fast and agile. We played rounders (like baseball), field hockey, and tennis. Once a year we had Field Day, to which our parents were invited. We had races, and my mom would hold my legs and help me practice the wheelbarrow race. I could jump my own height in the high jump!

We were not allowed to wear makeup, curl our hair, or paint our nails. One Sunday, Mommy curled my hair in rags for the Sunday school anniversary, and by Monday my hair was still curly. I was made to wear a cooking cap all day long in school, which was rather embarrassing.

Someone heard me sing in church and told my parents that I was a very promising singer. After that, I was sent by bus to Wednesbury one night a week for music and voice lessons. The very first song I was given to sing was "Bless this House, Oh Lord, We Pray." The second one was "How Lovely Art Thy Dwellings." This certainly was not what I wanted to sing professionally, so I stopped going.

Then Mommy wanted me to take elocution lessons to lose that, "Black country accent." I was finally realizing that my mom really was quite a snob. Not my dad, though. He would take his pitcher in the evenings to the pub for "three halves," as he called it. He would linger in the pub and have a bit of a chat with the lads, but Mommy was very jealous. She and Daddy had many an awful row, especially whenever Aunt Elsie and Uncle Ernie came to visit. They were Mom's brother and his wife, who didn't live too far away. Aunt Elsie liked to laugh and have a bit of fun, but after they left, Mom would start yelling at Daddy and accuse him of making eyes and flirting. Daddy never really said much of anything, but Mom would be cross for two or three days, slamming cupboards and doors and not speaking to us. It was pretty awful and scary.

One night after I had gone to bed, I heard them yelling. I heard my dad say, "Damn it, woman, I'm sick and tired of it. I may as well end it. I can never do enough for you!"

Next, I heard my mom scream, "He's got a knife"

I flew down the stairs, scared and crying and yelling for them to stop, but they didn't hear me. I pushed a chair up to the back door so that I could reach the bolt and open it. Then I ran to the neighbors' house, the Westwoods.

I screamed for Mr. Westwood to come stop my parents from killing each other. He went into our house and took the knife away and somehow settled them down. I was sent back to my bed, but I couldn't stop shaking and crying.

Of course, the gossip mongers all heard about it and blamed my mom because she was always so unfriendly, while Daddy was always so neighborly. Some of them said to me, "You poor girl, fancy having to live like that!"

I tried to tell them it had only happened that one time, but who listens to a young girl? I used to hear the poorer neighbors, who drank all the time, yelling and swearing and fighting—but they thought my parents were above that sort of thing.

I was never allowed to play with the neighborhood children except for the Powells and Joyce Westwood, and then only outside, never in my house or theirs. I was allowed to walk down to our neighbor Marie's, and I would push her son Peter in his pram down the street until he fell asleep. Marie was ever so grateful, as Peter was a sickly baby, and she didn't get much rest. But Mom told me I couldn't go into their house or anyone else's because they would pump me for information. They never actually did, and I became quite fond of Marie, her husband, Ike, and their daughter, Christine.

After the war started, things changed a bit. Everyone pulled together as the boys were drafted and the women went off to work in the ammunition factories. Air raid shelters were built, and we were all issued ration books and gas masks. My father had his own private shelter built at the end of the garden, so that was the last of my swing. Even though I was thirteen, my swing was my place to dream and think. The government issued corrugated steel sheets to those who wished to build their own shelters or if you lived too far from a public shelter. Ours was completely underground with a little potbelly stove and enamel teapots and cups. We had two long benches with pads, along with some blankets, candles, flashlights, lanterns, tins of food, and a first aid box.

I left Tipton Central school when I was fourteen to attend Wednesbury Technical College, which was a junior college, where I learned typing, shorthand, and other assorted office skills. Then I got a job at Horsley Bridge—but no matter what one learned, everyone started out as a gofer. "Go fetch the tea, go for the mail, go to the post office"—and in between, someone would show you how they wanted things done.

Two young boys, Denzel and Leonard, worked in the office too. Of course, by this time I liked boys. I took a liking to those boys, and the boys seemed smitten with me! We had lots of laughs when we could, but the older people in the office didn't seem to like us younger ones too well. There was no romance, as I wasn't allowed to date yet—or, for that matter, to even be seen talking to boys.

But soon, I was in love. I just knew it was love, and it was Marie's nephew, John Ellis. I'd known John for years. He was good-looking, well-dressed, and often rode his bicycle past my house. I took to standing in the front window just to see him. He and his mom lived three doors away from Marie in a really nice new house. His mom owned a drapery store in Dudley, and his dad was a professional soldier serving in India.

John was an only child, like myself, and he attended Tipton Central for boys. After the war really got bad, his mom sent him away to the country, away from most of the bombing. Lots of children were sent away—some to relatives, and some just to country homes where people would look after them.

By this time, I had become a Sunday school teacher in the primary Methodist School. I attended church in the morning, taught Sunday school in the afternoons, and went to evening worship. Sundays were different in those days. Shops and cinemas were closed, and you couldn't knit or sew or clean. The only thing Mom did on Sunday was make dinner, which always consisted of a beef, pork, lamb, or chicken roast with potatoes and vegetables.

During the war, we were each allotted four ounces of meat per week, so Mom was able to buy a twelve-ounce roast. We had fresh roast on Sundays and cold roast and mashed potatoes on Mondays. Tuesday was wash day, so we had eggs and rice or bread pudding. Wednesday, Mom made stew with the roast leftovers, with lots of veggies. Thursday, she rode the bus to Wednesbury and stood in line hoping to get some offal, which was not rationed. This would be hearts, liver, tripe, or sausage, but you could only buy one or the other so that as many people as possible could share. You could go to the fish and chip shop too—these weren't rationed, and fish mongers would make their rounds with fresh fish every Friday. Sometimes, Daddy would trade a horseshoe job for a leg of pork, and Mom would save all the bacon grease and lard to bake with. She was very frugal, but we were never really hungry.

During the years of 1941 and 1942, we stayed and slept in the dugout almost every night. Sometimes the sirens would go off before I could get home from work, so I'd run like the wind from the bus stop and Mom keep my supper warm on the little stove down there. We could hear the bombs exploding all around us. When the all-clear sounded, we would venture out to survey the damage and see who needed help. We were very fortunate, indeed, as the worst for us were some blown-out windows.

One night, I woke up screaming. I thought a firebomb was coming right through my bedroom window, but it was only the full moon shining in. I had forgotten to draw the drapes. Another night, the sirens blew in the middle of the night. We had decided to try to sleep in our own beds that night, and I jumped up and ran into my parents' room. It was quite comical. In his haste to dress, my dad put his trousers on backwards and couldn't find his buttons!

Some nights, the young people would venture out into the street and sit together on the wall across from my home. We would try to identify the Jerrys' (Germans') from our own planes.

One Sunday afternoon after Sunday school, a few of us decided to take a walk over the bridge to the small nearby park when suddenly, a German plane flew in really low and began strafing the play area. No sirens had been sounded, so we were not expecting trouble, but this lone plane had made it through without being detected, and it attacked.

I turned and ran for home, certain I was going to die. It is truly surprising how fast one can run when you're scared to death. I saw many children killed that day, and it is a haunting memory that I will always carry with me.

It was during this time that John Ellis came back home. He and his mom really needed each other. John was now a teenager, and the man of the house. I was so happy to see him, and he to see me. He had written to me while he was gone, and they were very sweet and loving letters.

We started walking out together after church on Sundays, and sometimes I would tell my mom I was going to Marie's or just for a walk, but I was going to meet John. Sometimes we would hold hands and walk. Sometimes we stood under the railroad bridge and he would kiss me softly and touch my breast. I had feelings I'd never had had before. My first love, my first awakening. Such tenderness always left me wanting more.

John said it was wrong to do anything more because we were so young and he had to go off to college, but that he would always love me. John didn't have to go into the service. His dad was overseas, and he was an only child.

Time passed by. I kept working and going to church and Sunday school, and John went off to college.

One Saturday, I took the bus to Dudley, which was a much bigger town than Tipton and had better shops. I needed new shoes, and because they had to be bought using our clothing coupons, we had to buy really good ones that would last a long time. When I got to Dudley, it was a little too early, as all the shops closed from noon to two. It wasn't quite two, so I decided to hang around and browse.

Here is where I have such a difficult time continuing with my story. I think it is because I came to a crossroads in life, and I still wonder if I made the right decisions.

As I was standing there waiting for the shoe store to open, an American soldier came up to me, smiled and said, "Hi."

I, of course, smiled back and said, "Hello."

He introduced himself to me, and I explained why I was waiting for the shop to open. He was very handsome. He told me that he was homesick, especially on weekends. So I invited him to come to our church service the next evening. I gave him the directions, the time, and the number of the bus to take to Gospel Oak.

I went to the evening worship, but he wasn't there. When I came out, he was waiting. He said that the bus had been late. I asked him if he would like to go home with me to meet my parents. Mother was mortified, to say the least—to think that I would bring a strange man into our home! But as the Brits would say, "She kept a stiff upper lip," and was coolly polite and offered him some tea.

We sat in the sitting room, getting to know all about Gail and his family. My dad reminded him that the last bus would be coming soon and he'd better be off. If he missed it, it was a very long walk back to Dudley. I walked Gail back to the bus stop, and he asked if he could come back the next weekend. I agreed and invited him to Sunday tea, then to chapel with me in the evening.

The next Sunday afternoon, he arrived at my home with a bag full of goodies. It was the American Army's way of being nice. If a soldier was invited to eat with an English family, he would collect the goodies from the PX (Army and Air Force exchange service) and take them to the host family. I don't remember exactly what it was he brought, but I know that it pleased Mom and Dad, and I was proud as a peacock to show him off in chapel. Everyone made such a fuss over him—the first American soldier they got to meet in person.

One weekend, I took him down to Marie's house. She was so pleased that she told him he looked like a movie star. Marie loved American movies and music. That evening was great fun, but we realized that Gail had missed the last bus to Dudley.

Marie said, "It's no problem, you can sleep on our sofa and my husband Ike will wake you up to catch the first bus in the morning."

By now Gail was kissing me goodnight, and we started courting—or "walking out," as we called it. On my seventeenth birthday, he gave me a silver necklace and told me that he loved me and wanted to marry me. I told him I was too young to marry, and besides, he had to go back to France and Germany.

I can't bring myself to give you the details, but he came over one night and told me he was shipping out. We walked down the canal and across the fields and finally sat down in a very secluded spot. Gail wanted to make love to me, but I was scared—scared of my parents, scared of the unknown, and scared of having a baby.

He was five years older than me, and he said, "I won't get you pregnant, but even if it did happen, it would be our baby."

No bells rang, although it really didn't hurt, and before he left for Europe, he gave me an engagement ring.

I took the bus to Dudley to see his company boarding trucks to leave. He ran across the street and gave me a dollar bill on which he had written, "I love you, Gail." We wrote each other letters for a year, but on my eighteenth birthday, I was required to report to the draft board. I had a choice to join the services or register to work in an ammunitions factory.

Chapter 3: Life in the Signal Corps and Falling in Love

I went home and told my parents, and my dad said, "It's the Army for you, my girl. You will have curfews and orders, so you'll be well looked after. If you go into the ammunitions, you'll have to go into the city, be billeted in a private home, and have no one to look after you properly."

So I reported to the Army and did my training in Edinburgh, Scotland. It was my very first time away from home, and I loved it. I loved the train and the marching, the uniform, and the free time when we could go into the city of Edinburgh to Princes Street and the Castle. I trained for the Signal Corps. The toughest part was the split hours—the night times killed me—but like everyone else, I got used to it.

One evening, I went out with my friend, Evelyn McKenzie, a Scottish girl with red hair and freckles. She persuaded me to go to the Palais le Dance on Princes Street. We took the bus into the city and to the dance hall. She loved to dance. It was mostly service people there, and many soldiers asked her to dance. A few asked me, but I smiled and said I didn't know how to dance.

A Canadian airman came and asked me, and I started to claim I didn't know how again, when suddenly McKenzie pushed me out of my chair and said, "All you have to do is follow and listen to the music."

Well, the tune was a slow one, "Sweet and Lovely," and the young man was Don Manion from Ottawa, Ontario. I stepped on his toes a few times and apologized, but soon I knew how to dance. Next thing you know, Don and I were dating. I didn't tell him about Gail, and he didn't ask.

I didn't wear the engagement ring, as Mom wouldn't let me. She was convinced someone would steal it. I wasn't in love with Gail and hardly ever thought about him now. Don used to call me when I was on duty, and he always said, "Hello, Sunshine"—hence my nickname, Sunny.

I was so petite, barely five feet tall and not even one hundred pounds. I was always happy, not a care in the world. The older soldiers used to tell me that I reminded them of their daughters back home, and they always seemed to want to take care of me.

Mac and I were transferred to York City, as our training was over, and now it was the real thing. One night whilst on duty, I got a call saying, "Hello, Sunshine."

It was Don. He told me he was stationed at an airfield close by and had a couple of days off. He picked me up the next day. We went canoeing on the river and then we explored the city of York. The only picture of me in uniform is the one of me sitting on the city wall, which goes around the city, and it was Don who took the picture. We were so happy together, and I missed him when he went off on bombing raids, as he was a navigator.

One day, he called and said he had two days off. He asked if I could I get off so we could go to Scarborough for the weekend. I don't know how or why my time off coincided with his, but I packed my suitcase with Army-issued striped PJs and a blue woolen robe Mom had sent me because she knew it was cold up north. I had no other civvies (civilian clothes) because they were not allowed in wartime. So off to the train we went. It was crowded with service people.

We registered at a hotel, then went into town for dinner and dancing. When we returned, there was a huge fire in the fireplace and couples sitting all around. Don had booked separate rooms, but as I remember the rooms were very small. He walked me up to my room and kissed me goodnight.

I put on my PJs, but it was so cold in that room, as it was March on the northeast coast, that I put on my robe and went to bed. I couldn't sleep thinking about the day's events and the cold.

Suddenly, there was a light tap on my door and a voice saying, "Sunny, are you asleep, can I come in for a little while?"

I opened the door, knowing it was Don.

His teeth were chattering as he said, "I'm so cold."

I said, "So am I."

My bed was no more than a cot, but I moved over and invited him to climb in and get warm. We started to cuddle and get warm, to talk and kiss, and before I knew it, we were making love. The memory of that night has never left me—such tenderness and loving words, and getting through the Army-issued PJs!

Don told me, and I believed him, that he hadn't planned on this happening. I assured him that it was fine and that I loved him, and that he made me very happy. The next morning, we strolled on the beach and through town, and he bought me a little lace collar as a memento of our time together. We kept on dating when he was off duty, but we never made love again—only hugs and kisses and dancing. God, I loved this man. And then the dam broke.

I was called to the CO's office one day and told that I'd been

31

given marriage leave. They said my American fiancée was on leave in Tipton, and we were to be married. Oh, my God! I hadn't given Gail a thought in ages.

I couldn't call home, as we didn't have a phone. I took the train home after sending a wire stating which train and what time I would be arriving. Gail was waiting at the station with a big smile on his face and a bouquet of flowers. I pretended to be happy to see him. What else could I do?

I asked my mom to come to my bedroom, as I needed to talk. I told her about Don, and that I didn't want to get married to Gail. She scolded me saying, "Don't be such a silly madam! He came all this way to get married, and you'll get over this other man. Now here's your engagement ring. Put it back on." Then, as she was leaving the room, she turned and looked at me and said, "You know, many a girl has been murdered when she cheated on her man."

And so arrangements were made for a very small wedding at St. Mark's Church. Mom borrowed my cousin's wedding gown, as we had no extra clothing coupons. My school chum, Ruth Boffey, said she would be my bridesmaid because she had a dress she'd worn for her sister's wedding. Mr. Jack Smith, a friend of Daddy's, stood up for Gail, and my cousin Tom was Gail's best man.

My dad had hired a limousine to take us to the church, and as we were leaving the house, Daddy said to me very quietly with tears in his eyes, "This is not the way I had planned your wedding day. It was supposed to be a horse-drawn carriage and a party afterwards, but you know… on account of the war, and all."

Everything was blamed on the war. Mummy had arranged a lovely tea with cucumber and salmon sandwiches, fruit, little tea cakes, and a small one-tier wedding cake. Gail's mom's picture was propped against a vase on the table, and pictures were taken to include her photo. She was a very pretty lady, and Gail was a little sad she wasn't there. Did I tell you that he was an only child?

We didn't go on a honeymoon. We spent our wedding night in my bedroom, and I hated it because Mom and Dad and the rest of them were still partying and playing cards downstairs. I felt as though everyone knew what we were doing.

I don't remember much about it. We had ten days before we both had to report back to duty. Gail went back to Europe and we wrote to each other, but I didn't see him again until I went to America fifteen months later.

When I got back to York, colleagues in my office told me that a young Canadian chap had called asking for me and was told I had gone off on marriage leave. My heart fell. I didn't see or hear from Don for a very long while. Then one day he called out of the blue and said he'd like to see me. My heart leapt, and I agreed.

We resumed our friendship after I explained what had happened. I told him that he was the one I loved. I didn't feel married. I seldom even thought about Gail except when I received a letter. It seemed all he had on his mind was sex—just sex and more sex. After listening to your dad's account of wartime encounters, I guess he was just a normal G.I.

Anyway, the war ended. Because I was married, I was demobilized and sent home. I spent my last day in the city of York with Don. Before he put me on the bus to head for the railroad station, we cried and hugged and kissed goodbye and promised to keep in touch. Don gave me his home address in Ottawa, Ontario.

The train to Birmingham was crowded with American G.I.s as well as English soldiers. Even though they had fought against the same enemy, the British soldiers expressed anger at the Yanks, accusing them of stealing all the best English girls.

I took a taxi from Birmingham to my home, as the train had

33

arrived in the wee hours of the morning. The taxi driver said, "Come on, ducks, sit in front with me. You're my last call and you look tired. Goin' home on leave, are ya? You're a mighty pretty girl to be out on your own."

I answered despondently that I'd been demobilized and was headed home. The streets were deserted at that hour, and somewhere along the way he pulled off the road. He put his hand on my leg and started to move it upwards. I got the message loud and clear and punched him in the face.

He backed off in surprise and said, "See here, girlie, I heard you Army girls were givin' out all the time. I thought we could trade your fare for a little cuddle."

I informed him that I had fare money and would report him to my dad, as I had his taxi license number. I wasn't as brave as I sounded, and I was shaking all over, but he turned on his motor and muttered, "I'm sorry, I'll take ya home. I suppose if I'd been a Yank, ya wouldn't have cared."

I never did tell Mom and Dad, because Mom would have asked, "What did you do to provoke him?" and I would have had to listen to a lecture. So life went on. I returned to work in an office, went to church, and taught Sunday school again. Marie told me she had been writing to Gail and his mother, but she also let me know that John Ellis had been very upset when he heard I'd married an American.

Gail's mother wrote to me and sent me some material to make a dress for myself, which I did with Mom's help. Then we went to a photographer to get a picture to send her with me wearing the dress. She wrote me that everyone was anxious to meet me.

Gail wrote, insisting that he missed me terribly and urging me to hurry my visa application. I traveled to London to get a passport and was told to wait until my number came up, as there was a shortage of ships to transport all the G.I. brides and their children to America. Truthfully, I didn't care if I ever went.

Chapter 4: After the War – Life in America

Mom and I resumed our weekly routines, with dinners and trips to the theatre, which we both loved. Aunt Annie resumed her visits, as her husband, Will, had passed on. He was one of the few people who had got along with my mom. Annie traveled from Birmingham by bus and stayed for two or three days at a time. She had to share my bed, but it was big enough, and she would tell me stories of her life with Will into the wee hours. According to Annie, he was tall and handsome with a fancy mustache, and she had loved him deeply.

Some of my other favorite people were Aunt Lizzie, my father's older sister, and her husband, Uncle Collin, who lived on a farm. We visited them once or twice a year. They lived in a long, low, whitewashed cottage with stone floors and beamed ceilings. Aunt Lizzie used to churn milk and make butter on a large stone verandah out back of the house. She would skim off the top of the cream as a treat for me into a bowl of fresh-picked strawberries. We'd have a huge Sunday dinner, everything homegrown and homemade. We would stroll around their grounds gathering nuts to take home. I always dreamed of a cottage just like theirs.

A favorite time there were the early morning walks along Willingsworth Road, along the canal and through the fields with my dad. It was beautiful and serene. We'd take a basket and pick mushrooms, as he knew which ones we could eat. The grass was still wet with dew, and the mist rose up from the ground. When we got back to Mom, she would sauté them and serve them with eggs and toast for breakfast.

At home, I loved to chum around with the Smith girls, whose parents were friends of my folks. Theirs was a jolly household with five girls and only one boy—so much livelier than my house.

I eventually received my sailing notice for March of 1946. Mom took me shopping for new clothes, and we bought my very first pair of slacks—blue linen, wow! Mom thought it might be chilly aboard the ship, so we also bought a beautiful white woolen coat. In London, I went to Lilyo and Sinners, a famous shoe shop, and acquired a pair of red Oxfords. I don't know how Mom accumulated all the clothing coupons, although she said she didn't buy much clothing during the war. Maybe she had been saving them.

As a going-away gift, she gave me one of her rings. Mom had saved my money from the Army, and she had always encouraged me to save part of my salary. I never had to pay for room and board at home, but I certainly had to put money in the bank. When I was ready to leave, I had three thousand pounds saved, but the government only allowed one to take two thousand pounds out of the country, as England was very poor after the war. Mom promised to send more once it was allowed.

At some time during these preparations, Don sent me a parcel. In it was a pair of black suede wedge shoes, a lovely sweater, and some tinned foods for Mom and Dad. Mom thought it was very kind of him to do that. He included a note that he was out of the air force and back home with his family. He hoped I was happy.

The day came for me to leave for America. I was sad, as I didn't want to go, but Mom insisted, "It's your duty as a wife to go."

My parents took me to the train station in Wednesbury, where I could get a train to London. I had left from that station many times to go on holiday, but this time I felt as if I was leaving forever. Mom didn't say very much, but Daddy cried and told me to be happy. I cried too and told them I would save money to come home real soon. Only now that I've experienced my own children leaving home can I understand what my parents must have felt. It would be more than five years before I would see them again.

I arrived in America on March 18, 1946, after six days at sea on the Queen Mary. It was quite an experience—so many young women and babies on deck. At one point, I was asked to help with the children, as many of the mothers were seasick. Luckily, I was not affected at all. We had an amateurs' night one evening, and I sang "It Might as Well be Spring." The captain gave me an autographed postcard, which is no doubt still among my many treasures.

I caught a glimpse of the Statue of Liberty in New York, but not much else, as we boarded trains to various destinations after we disembarked. I was bound for Chicago. I had a top-level sleeping bunk, and I recall lying there with the curtain pulled aside to drink in the beautiful full moon. I've always loved moonlight—it's so romantic. I lay there, wondering what my life in America would be like.

The next day, I arrived in the roar of Chicago. Gail was there to meet me, looking different in civilian clothing but still quite handsome with his toothy smile. I felt rather shy, as though he were a stranger. He was a very commanding, take-control sort of person. He insisted on a walk along the waterfront before we went back to the station to catch a train to Aurora, where he had left his motor car, a Model T Ford. He took a photograph of me standing on the running board. We drove to meet his parents, who lived at 73 South Lincoln Ave in Aurora. Why do I still remember that address so well?

Gail's mother was a very attractive lady, with a pretty face and silver hair, and she welcomed me warmly. His father was different—very forward and outspoken. He was a naturopath by profession and said he couldn't wait to give me a treatment. "Make you feel like a new girl," he said. Gail's Mom informed me that in the near future, she and Gail's aunts were going to give me a bridal shower. I had absolutely no idea what a bridal shower was.

Gail and I left to go to our own home, an apartment on Indian Avenue. It was in the 1100th block, in the Guzmans' apartments, on the second floor. (This was across the street from where your father grew up, and where we eventually raised our family). It had a joint kitchen and living room, and one bedroom—all very, very small.

Of course the minute we were situated, Gail couldn't wait to have sex. I was so homesick, lonely, and confused. Who was this stranger forcing himself on me? I was also tired. It had been a long and exhausting journey.

The days went on. He said he was enrolled at Aurora College under the G.I. bill. He didn't care much for my clothes, so he took me downtown to a new store called Arthur's and picked out some dresses for me. Then he informed me I would have to get a job because he was going back to school.

The first job I landed was on Lincoln Avenue at Northern Trust Insurance. I have no idea why they hired me or even what my duties were, but they thought I was cute, sexy, and awfully British.

But I really didn't like it there, so I applied at the telephone company on Island Avenue, near the library. They gave me a job right away because I had been a telephone operator for the Signal Corps in the British Army during the war. The only thing I didn't like about this job was working shifts, but otherwise it was pretty good. Again, I had to travel by bus, which I caught on Front Street.

Gail informed me that I had to put my money into a joint checking account to help with the rent and so on. He was away from the apartment quite a lot, saying that he had split classes at school and it was silly to drive back and forth. I was happy when he was gone because he expected sex day and night, and when I refused or told him that I had my period, he became angry. During one such episode, he pushed me and I fell down the stairs. Mrs. Guzman came running to see what all the noise was about, and she scolded Gail and led me into her apartment. I wasn't seriously hurt except for my pride, and of course, I was crying.

She told me she had heard all the fighting that had been going on and decided it was time I knew what Gail had been up to. It seems he had a girlfriend who had been visiting him at the apartment, and they had been a couple for a very long while.

Mrs. Guzman's niece and husband, a young couple who were friends of Gail's, confirmed what she told me. They said that if Gail and I were happy, they didn't want to tell me. Gail's girlfriend was a young schoolteacher who also attended the Methodist Church and sang in the choir with him.

Things soon came to a head, and Gail moved out. Mrs. Guzman said I could stay on in the apartment until I found another place. She took me to see Judge Plain, who said, "Divorce the son of a bitch." He asked if I had children or was now pregnant. I told him no and was given a court date for an instant divorce.

The sad part about this was that Gail somehow managed to turn all the blame on me in spite of the witnesses, and I had to pay half of the attorney and court costs, which left me virtually without funds. I made twenty-four dollars a week at the phone company and had to pay twelve dollars a week for rent.

One day, Mrs. Guzman sent for me and asked me to move out, as her sister from Joliet had just divorced *her* husband and was coming to live there. Oh, God. I wanted to die. I was alone and broke in this strange country, with no money to go back home—which is what I would have liked to do. I started making plans to move out, but I didn't know where to go.

I had become friends with Shirley, Mrs. Guzman's teenage daughter. One evening, we were sitting on the front steps when a young man came walking by. He stopped to say hi to Shirley, and she introduced us. His name was Bob. Shirley mentioned my dire circumstances. He smiled, and without any hesitation said, "I have some married sisters. I'm sure one of them would have room for you."

That was how I came to live with Helen—one of Bob's and Ernie's sisters—and Tubby. I had to share a room with their four-year-old son, Chubby. They also had a baby girl, Meredith. Because I was so young, I had to obey house rules. I was not charged rent, but I had to help with the dishes and the two children on occasions. I continued working at the phone company.

Bob and I went out on dates a couple of times. He took me to a carnival in Farnsworth, and once to a movie. Then his brother Ernie came to visit Helen. He had just returned from the war in England.

Ernie's first words after greeting his sister were, "I've come to check out the Limey."

I happened to be home at the time, and Helen introduced us with a big grin. I wasn't terribly impressed. I thought he was rather cheeky, and the way he looked me up and down, I thought he could see right through me. But he had a very disarming smile.

I had made friends with a young couple, Ginny and Charlie Woolnough, who lived in an apartment at the Guzmans'. They invited me to dinner once and introduced me to their friend, Ron. For Ron and myself, the chemistry was all wrong, but I did make a recording while I was there, saying hello to Mom and Dad, and I sang "Let The Rest of the World Go By," which was my dad's favorite—he'd taught it to me.

I have a picture of me holding a microphone as I made this record. My parents didn't have a gramophone, but they must have found someone who did, because they wrote back saying, "It was lovely to hear your voice again."

Ernie kept coming around and asking me to go out with him, but I had met another young man through Ginny and Charlie— Glenn Davidson, a sailor who had also just come home from the war. He was the one who took photographs of me sitting on Helen's front stoop and standing in front of the house.

Glenn was quite the photographer. I liked him—he was very funny—but that was all. He had a car and asked if I would like a ride home one night. I was working a split shift and would not get home until nine p.m. Lo and behold, when I came down from the operator's room, whom did I see waiting? Not only Glenn, but also Ernie. They had chatted together, not realizing they were waiting for the same girl.

They seemed embarrassed, but I thought it quite hilarious. (This had happened once before to me in England, when two boys had arrived to take me to the pictures at the same time. My father had scolded me, saying it was extremely unkind, but we all three caught the bus and went to the cinema together.)

I don't remember if I got a ride home with Glenn or with Ernie, but whatever happened, it did not deter Ernie at all. It was close to Memorial Day, and the Donka clan had a picnic at their ma's house. The five sisters and their husbands and children, Loui and Mabel, and the three younger unmarried brothers—Dave (fourteen), Bob (seventeen), and Ernie (twenty-one)—were all there. I was introduced to everyone, but Ernie's mother and other sisters (except Helen and Margaret) let me know in subtle ways what they thought of divorced women. They were staunch Catholics with not so much as a whisper of divorce in their families.

But Ernie was smitten and pursued me regardless. One night, Helen and Tubby asked us to babysit so that they could go out.

"I don't know much about caring for babies," I told her.

"Oh, there's nothing to it," said Helen. "If she cries, give her a bottle. If she wets, change her diaper. Besides, Ernie's been around lots of babies."

It was a disastrous night. Maribeth woke up, and we gave her a bottle. Ernie said, "You just put it in her mouth and prop the bottle up a bit."

Somehow, we didn't put the nipple on right and the poor baby got soaked. Thank heavens Chubby was asleep. All this time, it seemed, Ernie had it in his mind that because we were going to be all alone in the house with two sleeping kids and a convenient sofa that we were going to make love.

Helen was furious when she got home and saw the mess, and she accused us of having sex instead of taking care of the baby. Ernie tried to deny it, but Helen knew him only too well and thought the worst.

Ernie was very kind and understanding later when I started to cry and told him how things had been with Gail. I told him I didn't really like making love. Mind you, I enjoyed kissing and hugging—

just not the actual sex part. He promised me he'd never hurt me or force me to do anything I didn't want to do. And he kept his word, while continuing to see me.

It came to the point that he declared his love for me and said he wanted to marry me. I told him I didn't want to get married. All I wanted to do was to save enough money to go home. I had left my ring on Helen's sideboard, and Helen allowed him to take it to the jeweler to have it sized. Ernie went ahead and bought me an engagement ring.

In the meantime, I had written a letter to Don in Canada to let him know I was divorced. I waited eagerly to hear from him, but the letter was returned to me unopened and stamped "Refused." I was broken-hearted and confused, but I could tell no one. I never ever mentioned it. I felt ashamed and humiliated. I kept the letter for a while, but then I tore it up and threw it away.

One night, Ernie disappeared. Tubby later found out that he was at a bar with a buddy, getting very drunk on cognac. Tubby brought him home, and Helen made him drink lots of coffee. Ernie burst into tears and said he didn't care about anything if he couldn't marry me. What a dilemma for me! I had no proper job, no money, no place of my own to live. What was I thinking?

As I began to reconsider, I told Ernie that we would have to call my parents. But since they didn't have a phone, we had to call a neighbor, Mr. Westwood, who lived two doors down from them and was the only person I knew nearby who had a telephone.

We finally got through to him, and he kindly called my parents over so that I could speak to them. I didn't think I remembered what my mom said, but now it comes back to me: "Haven't these Yanks done enough to hurt you?" she said bitterly.

Daddy just said, "Well, my girl, as you made your bed, you must lie in it."

Ernie spoke to them briefly, but all I gleaned from that conversation was that he assured them he would be good to me and take care of me.

On Memorial Day of 1946, the Donka clan had another big party at Grandma Donka's house. It started early with breakfast, washed down with beer. Lunch was homemade bean soup, various dishes that everyone contributed to the picnic, and more beer. I was introduced to the few I had not met. Some were kind and friendly, others were not, and they still fretted, "How dare Ernie want to marry a divorced woman? Isn't he a good Catholic boy?" (Although he never actually went to church.)

That June, I celebrated my twentieth birthday. Helen baked me a lovely cake—she loved playing Cupid. The next thing I knew, Ma Donka was having a room addition built onto her house. With all the boys coming home from the armed forces, there were no rental houses or apartments to be found.

Helen took me to town to buy a wedding dress, something simple, and Ernie's mother and sisters put on a great big bridal shower at the 129th Club. All the family and the neighbors were invited, and the club was also booked for the wedding on Saturday, October 19th. Ernie and I went to Broadway Furniture to choose a bedroom suite, and the new addition to Ma's house became our bedsit room. Ernie had returned to his prewar job at Stephen & Adams, and I continued to work at the phone company.

October 19th was a perfect day. The sun was shining. My dress was very simple but pretty. When Ernie arrived at Helen's place, looking quite handsome in a suit and tie, he presented me with a pearl necklace, which I still have. Aunt Helen's friend, Eleanor, did my hair and threaded carnations into it, and I held a bouquet of carnations. The women wore corsages, and the men, boutonnières. The flowers cost a total of twenty-two dollars, and I always kept the florist's receipt.

We were married in Helen and Tubby's home by a justice of the peace. Bob was the best man, Julia was my matron of honor, Dolores was a bridesmaid, and Dave was the usher. After that, we went to Grandma Donka's house, then on to the Park Place Photo Studio for photos, and finally to the 129th Club for a grand reception.

Ma and the girls had made all the food: cabbage rolls, chicken paprika, sausages, potato salad, and lots of pastries for dessert. There was a band for dancing—it was quite a wild affair. We traveled to Chicago for our honeymoon, and you would never believe where Ernie took me: to a burlesque show!

A taxi stopped to pick us up, and when it arrived, he jumped in first and left me standing on the curb. I guess he was just excited, but that's how life with Ernie played out for the next fifty-five years.

I loved being a mother and a wife. It has been a truly great experience. I had many lessons to learn, and Ernie was a good teacher. We made mistakes along the way, but always with love. We laughed and cried and loved, giving comfort to each other in times of need. But our greatest gifts were our children. I guess I'd do it all again. I'd just do it better.

In the end, for a little girl who didn't know where she came from, I'd say I've done rather well, and my heart is full.

Mary's Story: Afterword

Mary's Birth Family
Mother: Eleanor Marguerite Cooper (7/10/1907–12/5/1933)
Maternal Grandmother: Mary Isabella Ritchie Cooper (1875–1921)
Maternal Grandfather: William Henry Cooper (1867–1925)
Birth Father: Hugh Larkins (9/13/1895–5/13/1979)
Paternal Grandfather: Thomas Larkin (10/4/1866–4/3/1924)
Paternal Grandmother: Annie Straney (11/11/1860–12/1/1931)
Half-Sister: Joyce Cooper (8/28/1929–11/10/2024)
Half-Brother: George Taylor (9/15/1931–7/12/2006)
Stepfather: Albert Taylor (9/28/1905–death date unknown)

Mary's Adoptive Parents
Adopted Father: Harry Dodd (1885–1961)
Adopted Mother: Agnes Elisabeth Dodd (1884–1957)

Mary Irene Cooper was born to Eleanor Marguerite Cooper on June 15, 1926. Eleanor, a domestic servant of 25 Frederick Street, Brandon, entered the Durham Poor Law Institution on March 13, 1926, where six months later she gave birth to Mary. Mary was listed as illegitimate. Both were discharged on October 10, 1926.

Records show they were readmitted on October 4, 1927, nearly a year later, and discharged four days later on October 8, 1927, into the care of H. Cooper of 23 Fredrick Street, Meadowfield. We do not have the identity of H. Cooper but assume a relative. (Eleanor's father was William Henry Cooper whom we believed died in June of 1925.)

We have no further information on Eleanor until the birth of Joyce Cooper, who was born in London on August 28,1929. Eleanor gave birth to George Henry Taylor two years later on September 15th, 1931, Eleanor was married to George's father, Albert Edward Taylor. We assume that Mary resided with Eleanor, Albert, Joyce, and George in Abbots Bromley in County Staffordshire, at least for a time.

Mary was admitted to the Lichfield Orphanage from the Durham Institution on July 22, 1932, she was six years old. The Durham Institution was also known as the Durham Poor Law Institute. We do not know when she first entered the Durham Institute, although from her memory I believe this was the first "orphanage" she writes about in her memoir, where she describes it as dirty, says they were not well cared for, and that she did not like living there. Records from Lichfield Orphanage show that her mother, Mrs. Albert Taylor—a domestic servant from St. Mary's Sanatorium in Abbots Bromley—and her stepfather, Albert Taylor, released Mary to the orphanage on this date, a year and four months before Eleanor's death.

Eleanor's death certificate states that she died on December 5, 1933, at 495 Outwoods Road, Loughborough. She was twenty-six years old and the wife of Albert Taylor, a general laborer. Cause of death was pulmonary tuberculosis.

Why was Mary in the Durham Institute, and why did her mother and stepfather release her to the Lichfield Orphanage? Was

Eleanor too sick to care for three children? Was it too much for Albert? Was Eleanor in a hospital in Loughborough?

Records show that Albert lived in Newborough with his parents, Samuel and Ada, his twin siblings, Samuel and Elizabeth, and Joyce and George after Eleanor's death. At some point, he must have decided to put Joyce in the orphanage, as she was released to Lichfield Orphanage on September 7, 1934, and he was listed as her stepfather from Newborough in East Staffordshire. George was raised by Albert's sister Elizabeth.

Mary's Birth Father, Hugh Larkins

This information comes from one of Hugh's granddaughters, Loretta Cannon: "My grandfather Hugh Larkins was a coal miner and married my grandmother Christina McPhee on May 28, 1921, in Hamilton, Scotland. Hugh and Christina had a son, Thomas, born in 1921 in Hamilton, and then a daughter, Flora, born in 1922 in Barra Island Outer Hebrides. When Christina was expecting, Flora said they lived in Hamilton, Scotland, but my grandmother left my grandfather when she was pregnant with Flora (we don't know why) and they were not together for five years. During this time, my grandmother lived with her parents in Barra, where Flora was born. When my grandmother's father died, my grandfather Hugh went to Barra and brought Christina back to Glasgow. We do not know where Hugh was during this five-year period—we just know he was missing from 1922 to 1926. As he was a coalminer, it is likely he was in Durham, as there were many collieries in Durham County. Hugh and Christina went on to have nine more children."

This information comes from Hugh's grandson, John Rosa, in the United States: "My mother, Marion, was the only one in her family to come to America, so my memories of Grandpa Hugh are from our visits in the late 1960s and early 1970s. He served in WWI from its beginning in 1914, where he was stationed in Africa. I asked him one time how old he was when he was in the Army, and he said, "I was a boy." He was a short man but had a lean, wiry build, probably from years of working in the coal mines. He always had a mustache and wore a tweed Donegal hat. When he was around the house, he would sit around the coal-stoked fire and smoke his pipe. And of course, like all good British gents, he liked to go to the pub a few nights a week. His family lived in Glasgow and was there during the Clydebank Blitz, when Germany bombed the city for two days in March of 1941. My mother, aunt, and uncle were infants at the time. After that, they moved to the town of Hamilton Burnbank. I would visit him at 30 Burnhouse Crescent, where he lived until his passing on May 13, 1979."

Mary's Half Brothers and Sisters (From Hugh Larkins)
Thomas Mark Larkins, 1/8/1921–1993
Flora Ann Larkins, 2/11/1922–6/25/2009
James Patrick Larkins, 2/27/1927–12/28/2000
John Vicent Larkins, 1/7/1929–6/5/2002
Francis Vincent Larkins, 1/29/1931–7/21/2021
Joseph Vincent Larkins, 3/18/1933–6/21/2000
Hugh Straney Larkins, 2/19/1934–3/1994
Cecilia Straney Larkins, 8/5/1936–4/29/2012
Marion Veronica Larkins, 7/5/1938–
Anthony Larkins, 1/15/1941–
Patricia Cavell Montgomery Larkins, 5/7/1943–

Mary's Adoption
Mary was discharged from the Lichfield Orphanage on March 3, 1934, and adopted on August 29, 1934, to Harry and Agnes Dodd

of Ivy Crescent, Gospel Oak, Tipton, County of Stafford, England. After Mary was adopted, Joyce was admitted to Lichfield on September 7, 1934, by her stepfather, Albert Taylor. Her mother was recorded as deceased. Joyce was discharged from Lichfield on September 27, 1935, to the care of Mrs. Boston, 55 Coventry Road, Kingsbury. Joyce and Mom followed a similar path in life. Joyce also married an American soldier and moved to Texas after the war. As I mentioned earlier, when we tried to tell Mom in 2017 that she had a sister living in the States, she became very angry and said she had no family other than her parents. In 2018, several of us flew to Texas to meet our Aunt Joyce and her daughters, Charlotte and Tony, as well as George's son and grandson, who flew over from England, where they still live—close to where Mom and Joyce were both raised. It was quite an experience, and very emotional. Joyce was a tiny lady and every bit as feisty as Mom. She was so happy to meet us all. I kept in touch with her up until her passing in 2024.

Letter to Mom from Aunt Joyce

My Dearest Mary,

I'm so happy to have finally found you! I've been looking for you my whole entire life. I don't have many memories of my early years, but I've always known you were out there somewhere.

I grew up in Kingsbury. I met a boy in the Army and came to the States in 1955. We settled in Texarkana, Texas, and I've been here most of my life. I have two girls, Toni and Charlotte. I always wanted a big family, as I was raised as an only child, but it was not to be.

Charlotte became interested in finding my birth parents, and the search began with a DNA test. We discovered lots of cousins I had no idea about, and I've been in touch with them. But finding a sister has the best gift I could ever get.

All my best wishes to you and your family for a blessed holiday.

With love,
Joyce

Mom's End-Of-Life Memory

What I do know is that at the end of Mom's life, she remembered a baby George, and that she worried about "who was going to take George." If she lived with her family until the age of five, she would have been old enough to remember baby George, and to know that her mom was sick and something was happening. Maybe Eleanor was too sick and could not take care of her. Maybe it was too much for Albert to manage three children. These are questions we will never have the answers to, but Mom remembered baby George, and Joyce remembered both a brother and a sister.

Here is the story about George. In June of 2020, I risked getting Covid for a second time and flew to my sister's home in Wisconsin to be with my mom. Cindy had called me and said Mom wasn't doing great and if I wanted to see her, I should probably make the trip from Colorado. I am thankful to this day that I did, as it ended up being the last three weeks of Mom's life.

After I arrived, we contacted hospice and they came in to help us through to the end of Mom's journey. During this time, Mom talked a lot about her past, and her mom and dad—the ones who had adopted her in 1934, mostly asking when they were coming for her, or saying she needed to go home to them as they were waiting for her. She also talked a lot about our dad, Ernie, who passed in 2002. She believed he was coming to get her and take her home, and she was ready to go home, wherever that might be.

At times, she seemed lucid and would tell my sister and I how much she loved us. Other times, she thought she was watching my brother David playing golf on the television! But one of her memories surprised us all. Alex's youngest child, Sienna, who was two years old at the time, would walk in and out of Mom's room throughout the day. But one day, it upset Mom to no end, and she kept looking at Sienna and asking, "Who is going to take George? Where is George going to go?"

At first, we were very confused as to what was happening. Why was Mom so worried someone was going to come and take Sienna away, and why was she confusing Sienna with this baby named George? Mom continued to get very upset every time she saw Seinna, until we finally had to stop Sienna from entering her room. We have no Georges in our family, so we were really confused as to who she was talking about. Then it suddenly dawned on me that she was most likely talking about her half-brother, George. Somewhere in the deep recesses of her mind, she had a memory of George. She would have been old enough to remember when her half-brother George was born in 1931, and as we now know this was close to when Eleanor became sick with tuberculosis.

Maybe Albert and Eleanor were discussing what to do with the children as Eleanor realized she would probably not be around much longer to care for them, and Albert probably realized he would not be able to raise three children on his own. Mom was transferred from the Durham Institute on July 22, 1932, to the Lichfield Orphanage. George would have been a year old. It broke my heart that Mom never knew she had siblings and a mother that loved her for the first six years of her life.

My mom's story has always fascinated me. When I was around twelve or thirteen, I asked Mom about her family. I distinctly remember her sitting with me on the couch and telling me her story of living in the orphanage and being adopted. She told me the whole story of Gail, and about her first love, Don. Mom had always believed that her birth parents had died in a car accident. She also believed all records had burned in a fire. I am not sure who told her this or where this information came from.

In 1959, Mom wrote to the General Register Office at Somerset House in London to find any information about her natural parentage. She received a letter back stating, "The Registrar General is precluded under Section 20 (5) of the Adoption Act, 1958, from furnishing information except under an order of a court competent jurisdiction." So she never received any information.

Mom, always known as Sunny by family and friends, died peacefully at my sister Cindy's home in Wisconsin on June 21, 2020, just days after her ninety-fourth birthday. She was surrounded by her daughters, granddaughters, and great-granddaughters.

Her life with my dad and his large family was filled with love and laughter, even though it was a bit challenging to go from being an only child, raised to be prim and proper, to joining a tight-knit, loud Hungarian clan.

She carried the pain of her early childhood quietly, tucked deep inside, rarely speaking of it. Yet, through it all, Mom faced life with grace and courage, always making the best of every situation. Her love for her husband and her children was boundless, and I will carry her love and the lessons she gave me in my heart forever.

As I conclude mom's story, I wonder about the day she was taken to the Litchfield Orphanage by her mother and stepfather.

Did she cry as she was handed over to some stranger? Did she cling to her mother? What did they tell her? Did Mrs. Campbell hold her and comfort her?

Mom never remembered that day in July of 1932. She always believed she had been in that orphanage from the time she was two years old. In reality, her stay in the orphanage was just over seven months. I can't imagine the trauma she must have felt to have buried it away for her entire life.

Dad (the smallest one) with some neighborhood kids

Mom with Dave Donka, Dad's youngest brother

Ernie

Sunny in England

The Donka clan (left to right) Dave, Frank, Mary, Bobby, Anna, Margaret, Ernie, Helen, Julia. Not pictured: Louis

Sunny

Mom and Dad's wedding

Dad's Army photo

Mom's first wedding with her father (second from the left)
and Gail (far right)

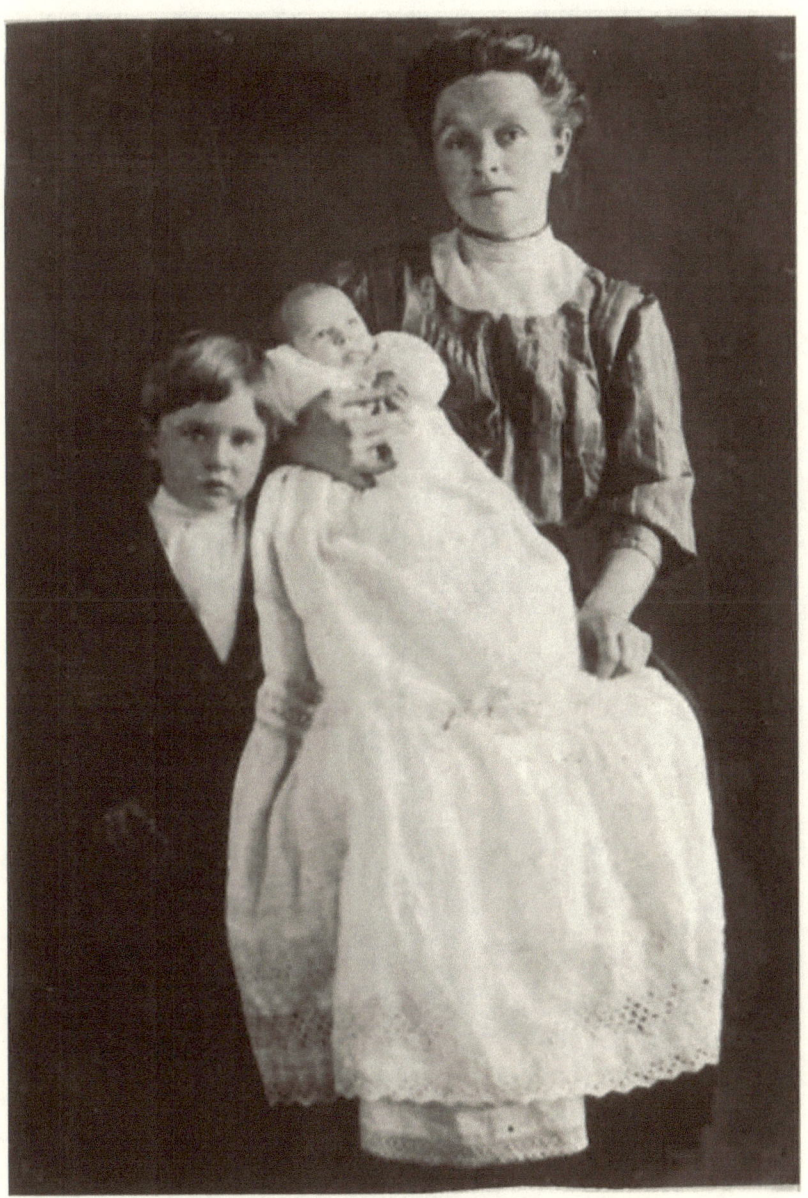

Grandma Mary Donka with Frank and baby Anna

Mom with Robin and David

Dad

Mom at her wedding to Gail

Ernie & Sunny
October 12th, 1996

Fiftieth wedding anniversary

Wedding party (left to right) Delores(Aunt Mary's daughter) Julia, Sunny, Ernie, Bob, and Dave

Mom and Dad

Part II: Ernie

Ernest Joseph Donka
Born: March 21, 1925
Died: May 11, 2002

When I leave this life—which I hope will not be for a long time—it will be biting, scratching, and fighting the whole way. I will not have much of a legacy to leave you. The best I can do is share my story, my memories, my love, and my sorrows. I have no way of knowing how long this will take, or when or how this will end.

Hopefully, you will enjoy my story and think of me always—for when it ends, I will no longer be with you in body, although my spirit will be with you all forever. Listen for me when sorrow overtakes you and you feel alone, as I will be there to comfort you. Close your eyes and hear my voice and feel my hand upon your heart. You have been the greatest and most loving family a man could ever hope for. I love and cherish you all.

Sometime in the fall of 1995, I noticed upon going to the bathroom that my stool was very black. This continued for quite some time until finally I went to my doctor. Subsequently, I went to five different hospitals and five different doctors, looking for the source of the bleeding. I had so many tubes up my rectum and down my throat that I dreamed a long black snake lived inside of me.

I also complained of a slight neck ache, and through the endeavors of my daughter Cindy, I was ordered to have an X-ray of my neck. A suspicious area was found in my second cervical vertebra. Soon after, I was given an MRI. A biopsy was taken, and I was diagnosed with plasmacytoma, a cancer considered curable two out of three times. It could also evolve into another form of cancer.

After twenty-four radiation treatments and almost a year of remission, I developed a very rare blood condition called Von Willebrand disease. This is when the blood will not coagulate, and even a small cut can bleed profusely. My oncologist, Dr. Chandra, was told to look for an underlying cause. After a bone marrow test, I was informed I had developed multiple myeloma, a cancer of the bone marrow.

It was a bit of a shock, but after a few minutes of deep contemplation, I thought how lucky I have been. I am seventy-three years old and have had a good and interesting life. I therefore put myself in the hands of the Lord. I have no fear of death. Whatever His will, I will bear my cross as He carried His for our sins. Whether I win or lose the battle, I shall do it with a happy heart.

Now for my story. Please remember who is writing this, and keep an open mind and have a few laughs.

The Donka Clan
Louis Donka, Hungarian, Jan. 21, 1887–June 6, 1936
Mary Donka (Kiss), Hungarian, Dec. 28, 1888–Jan. 11, 1965
Married June 20, 1908, Aurora, Illinois

Children

Frank Donka, March 20, 1909–Feb. 13, 1997

Anna Donka (Hanson), July 7, 1912–Oct. 2, 1996

Mary Donka (Johnson), Sept. 15, 1914–June 24, 2007

Margaret Donka (Bailus), Feb. 15, 1917–Oct. 27, 2008

Helen Donka (DesJardine), July 1, 1919–Nov. 25, 2003

Julia Donka (Baish), July 9, 1921–Sept. 3, 2004

Louis Donka, Oct. 26, 1922–Dec. 6, 1975

Ernest Donka, March 21, 1925–May 11, 2002

Robert Donka, Nov. 3, 1927–Dec. 13, 2010

David Donka, Aug. 17, 1933–March 25, 2010

Chapter 1: Early Life on Indian Avenue – The Depression

I was born on March 21, 1925, in Aurora, Illinois, to Louis and Mary Donka. My parents were Hungarian immigrants, who in those days were known as "Hunkies."

With five sisters and four brothers, I was the third youngest of ten children: Frank, Anna, Mary, Margaret, Helen, Julia, Louie (Duke), Ernie (me), Bob, and Dave. We lived at 1127 Indian Avenue in Aurora, directly next door to the house where I would eventually raise my own four children.

The house was a two-story brick-and-mortar with three tiny bedrooms downstairs, along with a kitchen and a small living room, and three small rooms on the second floor; eventually, one room became the bathroom. There was a dark and damp, scary basement—at least to a child—where the coal for heating was stored. When I was a young child, I slept in one of the upstairs rooms at the foot of the bed between my sisters Helen and Julia.

It was the time of the Great Depression. Men who lost all their money during the market crash of 1929 were jumping off tall buildings all across the country. My dad didn't need to jump. We'd never had any money and had always been poor. Despite that, we never went hungry because we were on what was called "relief." Once a month, a big truck pulled up to the front of our house, and we received a supply of staples: a huge sack of navy beans (I hated bean soup back then, and we had it at least once a week), a gunnysack full of grapefruit or oranges, a sack of prunes, and at least seven pounds of real butter. The butter was cut into one-pound triangles. This was the only time we ate real butter. We also received canned milk and canned Argentine beef (terrible)! Everything had a label on it: Not to Be Sold.

Once a week my brothers Duke, Bob, and I took our wagon to a store on Union Street, where we showed a card stating how many people were in our family. Then someone from a government truck passed out fresh vegetables—potatoes, carrots, cabbage, or whatever was available at the time. Then we walked to the Rainbow Bread Company on Highland Street, where we were given a loaf or two of whatever bread hadn't been sold in their store. We got fed pretty well by the government, and Ma and Pa raised chickens and rabbits to supply us with meat. Duke and I had to pick a daily bushel of dandelions to feed the rabbits. Needless to say, we never ate the rabbits when they were butchered.

During this time, if we needed shoes or clothes, we walked downtown to the Relief office, where we received a card listing the items we needed. Then we headed to the Aurora Dry Goods store to be fitted with new clothes. We made a daily trek to a store called Vassals on Dearborn Avenue, where we filled a gallon jug of kerosene for the lanterns and cooking stove.

The Depression was a funny sort of time. We were poor but happy. It was our life, and we knew nothing different.

My dad worked for the railroad. Every day, he got up around three a.m. to head to work. Summer and winter, rain or shine, he walked to the corner of Lincoln Avenue and Front Street and entered a tunnel that went under the railroad tracks. There he caught the train and rode it into the railroad yards in Chicago, where he worked on the railcars. In the evenings, he reversed his journey and came through the door around six p.m., where Ma heated up his supper. Before he ate, he went to the cupboard and pulled out a bottle of Palinka (whiskey) and downed two shots and smack his lips. Then he ate his dinner. If he wasn't too tired after supper, he would ask me to play a game of checkers with him. When I beat him, he called me a sly old fox, and every year I got a new checkerboard for Christmas. After the game, Dad went to bed and start all over again the next morning. How he managed to sire ten children was truly amazing!

We didn't have a bathroom in the house, or a bathtub—come to think of it, we didn't have a lot of things—but we did have a toilet that sat out in the open in the basement. It was scary to go down to the basement in the dark, so Duke and I instead peed into a sink that was in one of the upstairs rooms. Ma never knew.

On Saturday nights, Ma heated water on the kerosene stove and poured it into a round washtub in the kitchen, and then we all took turns bathing in the tub! We all used the same water, so you can imagine what the last person was washing in. Of course, the girls always got to go first, and I was positive that if they were mad at us, they did a wee in the water.

We had a long wooden tub in the basement, and in the summer, we carried it outside and put it under Dad's grape arbor and took our baths outdoors. The girls who lived next door—Marion, Jeanette, and Doris Urban—always peeked through the grape arbor and laugh at us. Duke and I didn't care and if Ma wasn't looking—we shook our Peters at them! We got even with them by peeking into Mr. Urban's bedroom when he was getting ready for bed and watching him powder his butt.

Always a big day for us kids was the butchering of a pig. When Dad bought a pig from a local farmer, Anna's husband, Whitey (Paul Hanson), hauled it home in his truck. Dad killed it and then burned straw all around it to burn off the hair. Frank and some of the older girls who were no longer living at home came over and carried it into the basement to be butchered. We younger ones fought over who got to eat the tail and the ears, which were mostly gristle from the smoke and fire, but we thought we had a great treat. Sausage was made and bacon salted, and meat was hung in Dad's smokehouse for days at a time. That's where the term "funny bacon"—also known as "klisa"—came from, which we cooked at family picnics when you kids were young. Dad often took it in his lunch along with a piece of rye bread and chopped onions. Great, huh?

One Christmas season, a man came to the door and told Ma to have all of the younger kids—me, Duke, Bob, Julia, and Helen—dressed and ready to go to a Christmas party the Saturday before Christmas. That Saturday, a big car pulled up at the house, loaded us in, and away we went.

First they took us to the Paramount Theatre, where we watched cartoons for two hours. Then we were taken to the Army Reserve building and served a big turkey dinner. After that, we headed to the Aurora Dry Goods store, where everyone was fitted with new shoes, pants, shirts, socks—and dresses for the girls, of course. Then we were taken back to the Army Reserve, where each youngster was given a large shopping bag. Accompanied by an adult, we walked along the long tables to fill our bags with toys, candy, nuts, and fruit. We were loaded down with so many goodies that the grownups had to carry the heavy bags. Bill's Hat Shop threw this Christmas party for the poor kids of Aurora. It was probably the best Christmas of my childhood.

At one time, before they had their own kids, Anna and Whitey lived upstairs in our house. Whitey had been traveling with the carnival when Anna met him. She persuaded him to stay in Aurora and get a job, which he did at a local door company, and they eventually married. But they often had rip-roaring fights.

One morning, we heard them fighting. Next, we heard Whitey run for his life down the stairs. Anna was at the top of the stairs throwing dishes, cups, and saucers after him. Ma told us to stay back so Whitey could get away. Whitey had the only car in our family, a black Chevy with a red pinstripe around it, but Anna had the keys—so Whitey quickly pulled all the spark plugs out so she couldn't chase after him in it. He didn't come home that night.

Actually, Whitey was very good to us. One Sunday, he told Ma to pack a picnic lunch and he drove us all the way to the town of Sheridan, which was thirty miles away. That was considered a long car ride in those days, and it was the farthest any of us had ever traveled. Once there, we had our picnic lunch and swam in the warm river the whole afternoon.

We had electricity, but we couldn't afford to pay the bill, and Ma told Whitey they were going to shut it off. But Whitey knew all the tricks of the times. He told her not to worry, that he would fix it so she wouldn't have to pay. He went to the basement and put a jumper wire on the meter so the electricity would come into the house but go around the meter so that it never registered. That did the trick! But he forgot to tell Ma not to let the meter reader into the house. When the meter reader found the jump and reported it, Ma was served with a notice to appear in court for stealing electricity.

Poor Ma didn't know what the heck was going on, so Whitey went to court with her. He told the judge he had done it to help his mother-in-law because she was poor and she had all those kids. He gave that judge such a hangdog story that the judge just sent them home. I think that judge was handling cases of people who couldn't pay their bills all day long.

The next day, the electric company moved the meter outside, right in the front of the house, and we went back to kerosene lamps. Ordinarily, this wouldn't have bothered us, but now when people went by and saw the meter outside, they knew we'd been caught stealing electricity. It wasn't long before almost every house in town had their meter outside. We were referred to as the "Electric Cheaters."

This was the Depression era, and there was no work in the country. When someone heard of a job somewhere, they hopped a freight train and bummed their way across the country to hopefully land that job. There were hobo camps popping up all along the railroad tracks. These men had to beg for food or clothing or anything else they needed. The railroad tracks lay just two blocks from our house, and every day we had one or two men knocking at the door asking for something to eat.

Ma never turned away a hungry person; she always found something to feed them. She noticed that these men passed by all the other neighbors and knocked on our door, so one day she asked a hobo why he'd picked our house. He took her outside and showed her a mark on the corner of the house and explained that if a hobo saw this mark, he knew it meant "Kind people will feed you."

Ma left the mark on the house, and so we always had a hungry man eating on our porch.

Life in the summertime was filled with activities that all kids liked to do: cavorting at the playground, swimming in rivers and lakes, and playing games like kick-the-can, run-rover-run, hide-and-seek, baseball, and *alle-alle-auch-sind-frei*. Sometimes, we went to the Copley playground on Wood Street and swam in the pool. To get there, we walked through what is now the baseball fields on Ohio and Indian Avenue, but back then there was a brickmaking factory. We skirted a big hole to get to the pool, but at some point the city authorities decided fill in the hole and make it a dump. Once they did that, we made out like kings!

We sat and waited for the city dump trucks to drop their loads, then we went through each fresh load of trash. When we found enough good treasures, we took our findings to Gordon's Junkyard and got a nickel or a dime—big money at that time! Then we used our windfall to go downtown on Saturday to the picture show. Every Saturday, the Tivoli Movie Theatre showed serial movies like *Flash Gordon* and *Tarzan*. Since the serials were continuations from the previous week, at least one of us had to fill the rest of us in about what had happened so we could keep up.

In the evenings, we sometimes sat on our neighbors' porch, and Mrs. Urban told us scary ghost stories, after which we ran like hell for home and remain scared all night long. The Urbans were good neighbors. Mr. Urban was a janitor at Oak Park School, which was just a few blocks away and where we all went to grade school. But because he held this job all through the Depression, they couldn't get free food from the government like us. So once in a while, one of the Urban girls joined us for dinner. That's just how it was.

On the corner of Indian Avenue and Loucks Street lived the McCoy family. Mr. McCoy was a nice man and always good to us. Once a week, he went down to the Fox River off Illinois Avenue, dropped a net into the water, and pulled up a catch of carp every fifteen minutes or so. Then he put the fish into a washtub and hauled it home, always bringing Ma five or six big ones. We ate a lot of fried carp in those days. If any of the carp had eggs inside, Ma cooked them up for Dad, who loved them.

Mrs. McCoy was a little mentally unbalanced. She would get all dressed up in white and walk down the street, talking out loud to herself, so we called her Crazy Mrs. McCoy. They had two older boys in their twenties, Roy (or Piggy, as he was called, because he was always greasy), a mechanic who fixed cars in his garage, and Ashley, who was always in trouble. Roy went to prison for robbing a streetcar conductor. He never really worked, even when he got out of jail. He had a glass eye and looked very weird and was the only person we ever knew who went rabbit hunting without a gun. He would chase a rabbit on foot until the rabbit started bleeding from the nose—then he caught it and took it home. Boy, he was fast and long-winded!

The Yuroks, who were German, lived to the west of us and had an older daughter and a son named Harold, who we called Speed because he could also run like a deer. Mr. Yuroks' hobby was building miniature ships. They were classics. Next to the Yuroks lived the Beaches: Paul, Roy, Frances, and Rex. Rex is in the picture of us kids wearing the funny-looking clothes, (that actually were our regular clothes.)

There were no other houses on our side of the street. Across the street lived the Mihalkas and the Tannenbaums. Mr. Tannenbaum worked in Chicago as a tailor. I can't remember what Mr. Mihalka did for work, but it was the time of Prohibition, and I know he made his own moonshine. In those days, you either bought illegal beer and whiskey or made your own. Pa made his own beer but bought his whiskey from his brother, Uncle Joe.

One time, Pa put too much yeast in the beer and the bottles exploded like firecrackers, scaring us all. One morning, Duke and I went down to the basement to use the toilet and found fifty gunnysacks filled with corn sugar. They were in big fat pieces and looked like the cuttlebones you would find in birdcages. We didn't know what it was, but we tasted it and thought we'd died and gone to heaven with this sweet treat. I put some in my pocket and took it over to Pauline Mihalka (she was my sweetie), who informed me they had the same candy in her basement but weren't allowed to tell anyone.

The next morning, all our candy disappeared! Uncle Joe had gone to Chicago the night before to pick up a load of sugar to make his moonshine, but federal agents spotted him and gave chase. Not wanting to lead them to his house, he shook them off his tail by bringing the sugar to our house instead. Ma gave him twenty-four hours to "get it the hell out of our house." He complied, and we were candy poor once again!

The last of the neighbors lived up the street: the Steibs, Boyters, and the Kalmans. They all had kids we played with. Mr. Steib was a barber, and every summer he shaved our heads. But he smoked a pipe and would spit on our hair before he shaved it, so we all came out smelling like tobacco.

Duke and I were always in trouble. We shared a bed in one of the upstairs bedrooms, and we didn't have regular blankets, so Ma made big feather quilts out of chicken feathers that we called dunhas. Duke and I got up every morning fighting. Ma would yell up the stairs and warn us to stop or she'd come sort us out. We never stopped until she actually came up those stairs to box our ears. I guess we never learned. (I chuckle here because years later, I had to do the same with Robin and David.)

One day, Duke and I went with Teet (Louie) Popp and Sy (John) Boyter to Fans' Park, which was a big park on New York Street and Farnsworth Avenue where they held car races, baseball, circus events, and all kinds of shows. On that day, we saw a carton of cigarettes through a car window, and Teet reached in and stole it. We each took four packs of cigarettes.

Duke and I knew not to take anything home because Ma would know that we had stolen goods, so we each buried ours and kept a few in our pockets. One day, I was talking to Ma when I reached into a pocket and pulled out a cigarette. I was wearing Duke's jacket, and boy did he catch hell from Ma. He never let me wear his jacket again.

Another time, Duke and I and some other kids went down to Indian Creek below the Ohio Street Bridge and went swimming naked. The overflow from the city sewers ran into the creek, so there was raw sewage in it. Trust Julia to walk over the bridge that day and see us swimming naked in the creek, and of course she told Ma.

Duke and I weren't exactly dumb, so before we went home, we rubbed dirt on our faces and hands, as we never came home clean. When Ma asked if we'd been swimming in the creek, we answered, "Oh, no. We were playing baseball."

She took one whiff of us and said we smelled like a sewer. She punished us by making us take off our pants and kneel on an ear of hard corn for an hour. Not for swimming, but for lying about it. Of course, we then hated Julia for squealing on us.

I should tell you about the time we all got scarlet fever. If there was measles, chicken pox, or scarlet fever in a house, everyone was quarantined. A sign was put on the house and no one could enter or leave. My dad was buying the house on Indian Avenue, where we lived, and the little house on Dearborn Street (where Bob ended up raising his family), but of course he lost both during the Depression. Frank was living in the Dearborn house with his boys when we got scarlet fever.

Pa, not wanting get scarlet fever, moved in with Frank and his three boys, so Ma had the chore of taking care of all of us kids on her own. What a woman! Old Doctor Boger told Ma that to stop us from scratching ourselves to death, she should rub our bodies with bacon! We were all greasy and smelled of smoked bacon, but it sure helped with the itching. My dad and Frank would sneak over at night and bring whatever supplies she needed.

Let me tell you about Pa—as much as I can remember. Pa developed stomach cancer sometime in the mid-1930s. I'm not sure of the exact year, but I think it was close to the time of the Great Chicago World's Fair. In those days they had no idea how to treat or cure cancer. My dad suffered a lot and spent most of his time in bed. He chewed Seal Snuff his whole life. This probably caused the cancer. He had terrible backaches and would have me walk up and down his back in my bare feet. He said it helped the pain.

The week before he died, he called me into the bedroom and gave me a dime and secretly asked me to go to the store and buy him a box of Seal Snuff. I didn't know what to do. I knew he wasn't allowed any snuff, but I wanted to get it for him anyway. I confided in one of my sisters, and she said to tell Pa the store was sold out of it.

He knew I was afraid to get it for him, but to this day I wish I would have gotten him that snuff. He died about a week later. He was forty-nine. I was twelve. In those days, the dead were laid out in the front (living) room of the home, and all the old Hunky women would come at dark and chant the rosary all night long. The men would sit at the kitchen table and drink whiskey and tell stories about whomever had passed.

I remember some of the men saying at my dad's wake that Dad was "a good man and a hard worker."

Chapter 2: Life on Dearborn Street

Soon after Pa died, we moved into the little house on Dearborn Street where Frank had lived. The building in front of us, on Ohio and Indian Avenues, was called the Romanian Star Club. All of the men in the neighborhood went there on Sunday afternoons to bowl in the two bowling alleys or play a card game called Shasta. During the week, there were very few customers in the club. The man who ran the bar and took care of the place was named Guzar. He was a fat old Romanian who wasn't too smart. When someone wanted to bowl, Guzar would send someone to fetch me to come and set the pins. I set the pins by hand, put a pin on each spot, and got the hell out of the pit so I wouldn't get hurt. I got five cents per game.

One night, two guys I knew came in with two girls. It was winter, and very cold outside. The guys were in their shirtsleeves, and the girls were wearing the guys' overcoats. They decided to bowl. So I went off to set the pins. Of course, you can't bowl with overcoats on, so the girls took them off—and believe it or not, they were both naked as jaybirds underneath! As you can imagine, two eighteen- or twenty-year-old girls bowling naked was quite a sight for a thirteen- or fourteen-year-old pin setter to witness. I probably didn't even charge them their fee. I'm pretty sure Guzar didn't, either!

Sometimes the young guys in the neighborhood—the Sabos, the Popps, the Boyters, and Bud Beverly—came in to hang out. Sometimes they brought with them a little comic book. It was a small booklet you could quickly flick through, and it was like watching a movie—like Popeye and Olive Oyl or characters like that—only it was a sex movie. We looked at it and then took it to Guzar, who sat at the end of the bar. As he was engrossed in that little dirty book, we had time to steal a bottle of pop and a candy bar and sneak out before he was finished. For shame!

Sometimes in the winter I went to the club and waited to see if anyone came in to bowl. One night I walked in at about six o'clock and sat down on a stool. Guzar was nowhere to be seen. I thought he might be in the bathroom. As I sat there waiting, Andy Cortez, a regular costumer who lived next door to my sister Julia and her husband, Ralph, walked in to get a beer. He asked where Guzar was. I told him I didn't know. So Andy went and got a beer, and we sat and chatted for five minutes. Then we looked at each other, and it dawned on us that we should look for Guzar.

We searched the entire building, but no Guzar. So we turned off the lights, locked the doors, and went home. The following evening, we returned, and there was Guzar. When we inquired about what had happened, he shrugged and said, "I had a real bad headache, so I went home." We asked him why he hadn't closed up the place, and he said, "I forgot!" I know this sounds far-fetched, but it's all true. They were the good old days.

Sabo and Bud Beverly used to be able to unlock the back door any time they wanted. This was still the Depression era, and there wasn't any work. These guys were around eighteen, and I was thirteen or fourteen. About once a week, they came by at night and stole a case of beer. Then the guys would sit around and tell lies to one another and drink the stolen beer. But they always took the empty bottles back, and that made Guzar happy.

One winter night when there was snow on the ground, Bud decided to steal a case of beer. He was already a little drunk, and he cut his finger. "I wonder how smart the cops are?" he said and left a trail of blood from the back door of the club to his house, which was right across the street. The boys sat around drinking, and then Bud went to bed.

One of the members of the club knew about the guys stealing beer, and he got mad and persuaded Guzar to call the police. The police went straight to the Beverly's house and got Bud up out of bed. Guess what he asked them? "How did you find me? Someone must have squealed on me?" And then he laughed. He only spent one day in jail. No one ever pressed charges for small things like that.

In a nearby empty lot, the neighborhood guys made a horseshoe pit where we played from morning until dark. If we weren't playing horseshoes, we played poker. Instead of using money (because of course we didn't have any), we played for farmer matches—cutthroat poker!

By the time the Romanian Club finally went broke, most members had died, so they sold it to the members of the 129th Division of the First World War, whose members lived in Aurora. They were a pretty good bunch of guys who supported a baseball team called the 129th Vets Team. I was the bat boy and hung around with the players.

I also tended bar at the club when I was sixteen, from 3:30 to 5 p.m. every weekday. The night bartenders, Bill Russ and Red Ertz, were WWI vets who also worked regular jobs.

Every day after school, I went to the club, opened it up, washed glasses, filled the beer tanks, and cleaned the bar area. I also served anyone coming in for a drink. I knew most of them, so it wasn't a problem. Anytime a dressed-up stranger walked in, I picked out one of the customers I knew and said, "Okay, the glasses are all washed." This was code for them to come and bartend. If I had been caught serving liquor as a minor by an inspector—and there were many of them—the club would have paid a hefty fine and might have been shut down.

Of course, my buddies from the neighborhood took advantage of the slot-hand pinball machines. One small penny slot machine sat on the counter. If no one was around, we turned it upside down and shook the pennies out. Then we traded them in for nickels and played the nickel machines. Soon, the penny machine was jammed, and they tossed it. But that didn't stop us. We noticed a small pin behind the pull lever of the slot machines. To pull the lever, you had to insert a nickel to push the pin down. We drilled a tiny hole in the side of the machine so we could use a stiff wire to depress the pin and play for free. We made a little spending money for a while. But alas, all good things end too soon. When they discovered what we had done, they plugged the hole and checked it every week.

Barney Poss, a local Mafia type, owned all the machines. Once a week, his man came in, took the money out, and split it 50/50 with the club. That man was Harry Tannenbaum, whose parents lived across the street from our house on Indian Avenue. One day, Sy Boyter, Louis Popp, and I hatched a plan. Popp's mother made her own soap, which was nice and soft. His job was to steal a bar of soap, and Sy's job was to watch and see which key Harry used to open the slots. My role was to lean on the table and talk to Harry, hiding the key from his view.

Sy pointed to the key, and Popp made an impression on both sides of the bar of soap. In two days, we had our own key to the cash boxes of three slot machines. Voila! Spending money again! We only took a little out of each box, but they soon noticed a drop in profits and changed the locks. Foiled again.

The pinball machine took a little more ingenuity, but we figured it out. There was a frame of wood around the glass of the pinball machine so that if the glass broke, it could be taken off and replaced. The wood was screwed in tight with putty so that the screws didn't show. Well, we took care of that. We dug the wood putty out of the bottom piece and replaced the screws so that we could slide the glass off and put the ball in the winning hole and win every time. Voila! Spending money again… Until one night, some drunk leaned on the machine, grabbed the wooden frame at the bottom of the glass, and fell back with it in his hands. Foiled again. No more machines. That was why I turned honest.

Well, not completely honest. We knew exactly what night the truck that supplied the potato chips, popcorn, and snacks came in. We also knew that the driver never locked his truck, so we would help ourselves to a few goodies. Duke and I could only take what we could eat because if we went home with our snacks, we'd have to convince Ma that we didn't steal them, and we knew we couldn't do that.

One night, we stole two dozen toffee apples. Duke and I ate two each and let Sy and Popp take the rest. They could lie and get away with it, but Duke and I were too honest!

Let me tell you about Uncle Gus and Aunt Maggie, and Uncle George and Aunt Josephine. Gus and George were Pa's brothers, who both lived in Chicago. Gus was a roofer and George a shoemaker. They both spoke fairly broken English. Gus was tough as nails and hated cops, calling them "cake eaters." Whenever he came to our house, which was usually on a Sunday when Ma was cooking dinner. He would come in smiling and grab Ma and give her a big hug. He called her "Mary, Mary, Big Strawberry."

When we heard Uncle Gus arrive, we all ran to him because he carried a pocket full of small change. He'd throw a handful in the air, and we'd run around and find what we could. Then we headed to the store on Front Street and got a little white sack of two-for-a-penny candy. We sure liked Uncle Gus, even though he was a pretty heavy drinker.

One day, Ma opened a quart of hot peppers. Uncle Gus asked if they were really hot, and she said, "Try one."

"Oh, no, I'm thirsty," Gus said and grabbed the jar, tipped it up, and drank half of the liquid. "Oh, my God!" he yelled, slamming his fist right through the plastered kitchen wall. Then he laughed and said, "You're right, Mary, they're hot."

Uncle George was different. He was tight-fisted and never gave us anything, but he always expected to be fed when he came. After Pa died, George would call Whitey and tell them he was coming over on Sunday to go fishing. Usually, Anna would invite me and Bob to fish with them, and make us a picnic with sandwiches to take along.

One Sunday when we went finishing in North Aurora, Uncle George said, "No sandwiches for me and Josie. We brought our own fried chicken. Josie, get the chicken out."

Aunt Josephine was meek as a church mouse, and Uncle George ordered her around like he was a king. Josie went to the car but couldn't find the chicken. They'd left it at home. George was mad as wet hen and blamed her. We didn't dare laugh out loud, but we sure enjoyed his misery.

Clarence Johnson, who was married to my sister Mary, joined a parachute club. He was always interested in flying. One winter, he was set to jump out of airplane over Fans Park on New York and Farnsworth Streets. He was supposed to come down dressed as Santa Claus. The park was full of people and kids waiting expectantly. We heard the airplane flying above, but it was too cloudy to see it. Clarence wanted to jump, but the pilot wouldn't let him. It was so cloudy that he was afraid he'd miss the park. A lot of disappointed parents and kids missed Santa that day.

Around this same time, there was a park on North Lake Street called Exposition Park. It had a huge swimming pool and diving board, a roller coaster, and amusement arcades. One day, Clarence and Whitey took us kids to the park for a day of big aerial performances. It turned out to be a very unlucky day. There was to be a balloon launch, and a man was set to go up and leap out of the basket with a parachute. As the balloon filled with hot air, it caught fire. Everyone ran. The man in the basket luckily managed to jump out and escape getting burned.

Then, two World War I airplanes simulated a dogfight in the air. As they landed, one of them crashed, but the pilot was only slightly hurt. In the big swimming pool, a man dove off the eight-foot tower and broke his neck. A young boy was killed when he fell out of the roller coaster. But the worst and last tragedy of the day was the lady parachute jumper. She asked Clarence to take her place because the pilot felt she couldn't do it, but he'd made a promise to Mary that he'd never parachute jump again, and he felt obliged to decline.

We were in Whitey's car, parked against the fence of a plowed field, where she would land. We saw her come out onto the wing three times, prepare to jump, and then go back into the plane.

Clarence said, "Something isn't right." She came out a last time and launched. As she was falling, Clarence shouted, "She's not going to open her chute!"

We jumped into the car and drove straight through the fence into the field where she landed. A man was waiting there to help her land the parachute. When she hit the ground, he grabbed the unopened parachute and tried cover her up. We were the next people on site, and it wasn't a pretty sight. Her body was all broken up and she had her fist jammed in her mouth as if she'd screamed the whole way down. Clarence never did do another parachute jump, and I wrote a school paper about that tragic day at the park.

At that same Exposition Park, they held what they called walkathons on a big dance floor. Couples would enter, and they'd walk and dance day and night for four days until only one couple was left standing. But you could sit and watch, and usually one partner would doze with their head on the other's shoulder while still keeping pace. The spectators cheered their favorites on, but it was hard to see couples just collapsing to the floor and be carried off. They did all this to win prize money.

Chapter 3: My Time in the Army

When I was in high school, I didn't really care for school and never did my homework. I tried out for football, but I was too small, so I got on the wrestling team. I weighed 105 pounds and was nicknamed Monk the Mangler. I won a few matches and lost a few. But I kept going to school until Sunday, December 7, 1941—the day the Japanese attacked Pearl Harbor.

Soon after that, Duke was drafted into the Army, which left Dave, Bob, me, and Ma at home with no one working. I quit school and went to work at Stephens & Adams Factory, supporting us on $1.75 an hour. I ran the machines and worked in the bearing department. I was fifteen at the time and working night shifts, which I hated, but I had no choice. Someone had to support us.

I worked at Stephens & Adams until I was eighteen. In 1943, I got drafted and went to Chicago for my physical exam, where I learned I was fit for service. At my interview, I was asked which branch I would prefer.

"The Marines," I said.

"The Marine quota is full."

"Okay, I'll take the Navy."

"The Navy quota is full."

"So the Army is all that's left?"

"That's right," they said. "You're in the Army."

Some choice!

I was sent to Camp Blaw in Florida for seventeen weeks of basic training. I weighed a fat 133 pounds and was really out of shape. On my first day, we went on a seven-mile march in the sand carrying full field packs. I thought for sure they were trying to kill us. When we got back and were dismissed, we all dropped right where we were. But little by little, they got us into shape, and by the seventeenth week we marched 28 miles at night with full field equipment.

By then, I was down to 110 pounds with not an inch of fat on me. I was lucky—I could maintain the marching cadence perfectly and was made the company guide. This meant I led all platoon marches. The poor guys marching at the back would constantly slow up and space out like an accordion. Then the sergeant would yell to close ranks, and they would have to run to catch up.

Our sergeant was a full-blooded American Indian who could do one-arm push-ups. He was an expert at jujitsu, and he always picked me to do demonstrations on. One day, he instructed me to fix my bayonet onto my rifle. Then he faced me and ordered me to charge him and run my bayonet through his chest.

I made a couple of charges but always stopped before I got too close. He finally said that if I didn't charge on a full run and do what I was told, he would run a bayonet up my ass. So I said, "Okay, Sarge, here I come."

I charged as fast as I could with my bayonet aimed at his chest. The next thing I knew, I was flat on my back. My bayonet was in his hands with the point against my throat. He sure was good, but I finally got him. One day after supper, I walked into the company area. The sergeant came out of the non-com billet and said, "Hey,

Donka, come here."

I thought, "Oh, shit, now what's he going to do?" I could see he was relaxed and didn't expect me to try anything, but I got brave. I approached him and said, "What's up, Sarge?" Then I put my hands on his shoulders, grabbed his shirt, and reeled backward with my foot in his stomach, heaving him over my head. Then I got up and ran like hell.

Sarge eventually caught me, patted me on the back, and said he was surprised and happy that he'd taught me so well. We became good friends after that.

Once we graduated from basic, we were scheduled for interviews. Louis Croie from Aurora was always my partner, and when ours came up, we were asked to join the paratroopers. We both said, "No way," but offered to join the mountain troops.

The sarge asked us how well we could ski, and we admitted we'd never been on skis in our lives. He said, "Get the hell out of here, you're going to Infantry."

After a short leave to go home, we traveled to Fort Dix in New Jersey, where we received all the equipment we would need. Within a week, we boarded a ship that had been a luxury liner, the *Miss America*. At this time, all ships going overseas were in convoy, protected by U.S. warships, cruisers, destroyers, and so on.

We were told that because of our speed, no submarine could catch us. The only way they could torpedo us was by plotting our course and lying in wait. So we zig-zagged across, a longer but safer route. It took nine days to get from the U.S. to England—nine days of throwing up for me. I got in the chow line one time in those nine days and got sick before I could eat. I lay in my bunk only one night. Then I grabbed two blankets and headed for the deck for the next eight nights, only leaving it to go to the toilet.

There were always sailors on deck with listening devices in their ears to hear if any submarines were around. Not one single light was allowed on the ship after dark. Three or four times, the loudspeaker came on and we were told, "No movement on board ship. No toilet, no scratching, no talking, no coughing, complete silence." The ship stopped dead in the water. This meant there was a submarine in the area, and we had to wait for it to pass.

After nine days, we disembarked at South Hampton, England. I was probably twenty pounds lighter but glad to be on dry land. We were sent to a replacement depot for more equipment and training. About a week later, we were issued everything an infantryman would need to go into combat and put onboard a ship and headed to France.

We were informed that we would follow the front lines of the fighting but remain two miles behind. Every day, names were called, and if yours came up, you joined a company and division on the front. When a company lost men, they called and asked what heavy weapons and types of soldiers they needed—machine gunners, riflemen, and so on. I was a rifleman.

We got to Omaha Beach about thirty days after D-Day. On D-Day, because there was no natural harbor on Omaha Beach, the Navy hauled a lot of old ships away and sank them a mile or two from shore to make space for the assault troops to get to shore. When we arrived, they threw a huge net over the side of the ship, and we were told to loosen our straps and go down the nets into small landing crafts. If we fell or missed our step into the smaller craft, we were to get out of our equipment otherwise we'd sink straight to the bottom of the ocean.

It wasn't easy climbing down that net with about 150 pounds of equipment on your back. No one fell, but a few guys broke their ankles jumping into the landing boats.

I didn't get sick going across the channel, but I did get sick while going to the shore in the landing craft.

I know that the guys on D-Day had a hell of a time on Omaha Beach. The Germans were sitting behind a big hill and the G.I.s had no cover on the beach. It was a massacre! A few miles from the beach is a cemetery for the First and Second Armored Divisions that were killed in the landing. You cannot see the end of the rows of white crosses from one end to the other.

When I landed, the fighting was taking place in the hedgerows. Each farmer in France marked his fields with a real thick hedge, so the Germans used these hedges to hide in and fight from. The G. I.s had to fight from one hedgerow to the next. There was one central town in this area that held the main German force. It was Saint-Lô, a good-sized town, and the American Air Force made the first big bombing of the war there. When I went through the town, not a single building was left standing. It was completely wiped off the map. That ended the hedgerow fighting in France. The Germans were retreating. We marched through France into Belgium, always a couple of miles behind the front.

The first place we stopped in Belgium was in a big park in some town. We dug shit trenches (toilets) and put canvas around the area so we could have a little privacy. All the townspeople came out to welcome us and walked right into our toilet area. Have you ever had to go to the toilet while you were out camping? Well, there I was squatting down, and a pretty Belgium girl came in and offered me a bottle of wine. Talk about bashful bowels! What an experience.

That night, the girls of the town came to our tents to really welcome us. War behind the lines was really hell. We could always hear the shelling going on and see the tracer bullets from the machine guns. In addition, every night a low-flying German plane (we called him Bed Check Charley) flew around looking for a

93

target. He only carried one bomb, but more than once he made us hit our holes when we heard the bomb dropping, and every once in a while a German fighter would fly over the tree level and strafe us. You can't hear a fast plane when it comes in at treetop level. It's on you before the sound reaches you. I dove in many a hole—mine or somebody else's—when I heard the machine guns going off as the planes flew over.

It wasn't long until one evening at roll call my name came up and I had to pack up because I was moving to the front with the 30th Division, 117th Regiment. Six of us were put on a red ball truck. All the drivers were Black guys, but they sure could drive and dodge shell bursts. Our driver took us to the edge of a small town, and we got out because it was getting dark and the Germans shelled the towns at night.

Our lieutenant met us there and said he didn't want us going to the front lines at night and digging holes in the dark. So we slept in the basement of a bakery, where we heard shelling all night long. In the morning, he returned and asked if anyone was hurt. I asked him how we could have been hurt, and he told us that the bakery had been hit with three shells that night. I told him I thought the sound had been our shell going over.

The lieutenant said, "By tonight, you'll be able to tell incoming shells from outgoing shells." How right he was.

When we got to the front line, we were told where to dig our holes. The lieutenant said we would not be moving for a few days and should try to build a cover over our holes to protect ourselves from shell shrapnel. Well, there was an old fence about fifteen feet ahead of me that had some old fence posts. I figured I could pull out two or three and build a nice top for my hole.

Now, when you hear an incoming shell, the longer you hear it, the farther away it is. I went to the fence and was shaking away at the pole when I heard an incoming shell. I ran and jumped into my hole, where I waited for more shells but heard none. So I returned to the fence.

Just as I grabbed the post, I heard another. This one was closer. I returned to my hole, and the shell went off much nearer than the first one. Again, I waited for more shells, but none came, so I went out again. This time, I didn't even get to the fence when I heard a shell coming in real close.

I took off and dove headfirst into my hole. The shell exploded pretty close by. I waited again. No more shells. I started to get out of my hole, but the guy in the next hole shouted, "If you start for that fence again, I will shoot you, you dumb rookie! Who the hell do you think they're aiming at? That German artillery gun is trying to zero in on you. Stay in your damn hole and live awhile!"

It didn't take me long to learn that the Infantry sometimes stayed in one place for a week or more. We were in a holding position, learning how to carry satchel bombs to blow up German pill boxes at night. The rule was: for every two manholes, one man stood guard, awake all night.

One night at about one in the morning, when I was standing watch with my eyes on the front, the bright moon went behind some small clouds and I saw shadows moving toward us. I kicked my partner awake and told him the German patrol was approaching.

We alerted the whole line, hearing all the guys loading their gun chambers, and waited. Finally we heard cow bells, and a couple of cows came into view. I had to duck into my hole because there were so many sleepy, mad, bitching Infantry men glaring at me.

To teach me a lesson, the next night I was put on outpost duty. Outpost is when a man is put between the front lines in no man's land. Before dawn, the lieutenant took me out to a camouflaged hole in no man's land. I was instructed to not lift my head out of the hole but to sit and listen all day. If I heard Germans trying to sneak up on us, I was to fire a whole clip of ammo out of my hole as fast as I could to alert the guys behind me. From dawn to dusk, I sat in that hole with nothing to do.

The only thing I saw was a bunch of American bombers fly over on a bombing mission. They flew through a lot of anti-aircraft fire. The only sound of war that I didn't miss hearing from my location was the sound of anti-aircraft fire when it exploded. It makes a sound like *crack-crack*.

Unfortunately, I saw one bomber explode in the air and go down in flames. Another was smoking and going down, and I kept saying, "Come on, guys, bail out." I watched it all the way down, but not one parachute came out. When the bomb run was over, the bombers came back, but they weren't in formation, and there were a lot missing. One plane was way behind the others and coming slowly. There were flak bursts all around that poor plane, but he just kept coming. I kept saying, "Come on, come on." I don't know how he did it, but that plane finally crossed our lines, and I cheered for him.

When it got dark, I was relieved and got the hell back to my regular hole. I tried not to screw up anymore because outpost is for the birds.

That night, it was our squad's turn to go into no man's land to lay an ambush patrol. The Germans had been sneaking into our lines at night and raising hell. We thought we knew where they were getting through, so eight of us removed all of our equipment except guns and ammo and crawled out to no man's land on our bellies and formed a big U shape.

A B.A.R. (Browning Automatic Rifle) gun was at the closed end with riflemen along the sides. The idea was to let the German patrol walk into our U formation, then we'd fire at them from three sides.

We lay out there all night without a sound. Just before dawn, we crawled back to our lines, but we must have been spotted by the Germans. The following night, another squad went out, but the Germans were there first. Our guys got shot up pretty bad. That was the end of ambush patrols for us.

But I have to tell you about our sergeant. He could sing like a bird but stuttered when he talked. Coming back from patrol one night, we heard a tank pull the bolt of a 50-caliber machine gun to start firing. An American voice called out to give the night's password. Each day, a new password and countersign were issued. If you were challenged, you either spat out the password or you were shot. When the tanker called for the password, out sergeant started stuttering. The whole squad yelled out the password. We then told him, "You sing, we'll do the talking."

The Germans were pulling back to better positions, so our lines moved up. I dug a nice hole and lengthened it so that I could lie down to sleep and left just a small hole to look out of. I lay down on my back with the covered part over my head. When it was time to stand watch, I sat up and moved to the open end of the hole. One night, I had rolled onto my belly while sleeping. When I was called to take my watch, I went to the wrong side of the hole and couldn't find the opening. I thought I'd been buried alive and started yelling for help. My buddy pulled me out by the feet, laughed, and called me a dumb shit.

That buddy was a full-blooded Indian (Native American) built like a tank. He carried a B.A.R. gun with twenty-four bullet clips. It was rapid firing and took a strong man to carry and fire it, wearing two bandoliers of cartridges. He had a special pack that he wore and could really fire this gun. I was his ammo bearer, and he the gunner. I weighed 115 pounds, and my pack and his extra ammo weighed about 100 pounds.

One day, I asked him to change packs with me and let me be the gunner. We swapped packs, and he put his on my back. I dropped right to my knees and couldn't get up. I promised him I'd let him be the gunner if he took his pack back. He had a good laugh at that, and I gained more respect for him. I don't know how he ran during an attack carrying all that weight.

One morning, the cooks came with the chow. We usually got hot K-rations like canned stew, hash, or chili. Other times, it was cold K-rations with dry hard cheese, candy, and cigarettes. This particular morning, we got steak sandwiches, which meant we were going to attack the German lines. It was like giving a prisoner his last supper.

Not too many guys could eat knowing what was coming. It wasn't long before we got orders to pack up all extra gear and personal belongings. Then we were told to draw hand grenades, bandoleers of ammo—and for me, a pouch of B.A.R. rounds. They said there would be fifteen minutes of artillery fire, ten minutes of fighters dropping bombs, and then we would push off to hit the Germans, some in pill boxes. Finally, we got to shove off. Immediately, there were incoming artillery shells.

During an attack, every time you stopped moving, you started digging a hole. This was because you never knew if you would stay or keep moving. Many times, you dug a little and then got order to move on with the attack. They informed us that there was a small creek ahead where the combat engineers would rig a small bridge so we wouldn't be bogged down. The first German shell knocked it out, and we had to wade across the creek under fire.

On the other side was a field about a hundred feet wide followed by a small grove of trees, and then a railroad embankment. At this time, we were in General Patton's army, and he pushed the Infantry so hard that our artillery and supplies could not keep up. They said the field was wide open, but there were German snipers at each end. All we could get were six artillery shells each to try and knock them out.

We had to cross the field to the grove of trees one at a time and as fast as we could. When my turn came, I took off like a scared rabbit. I saw and heard shots all around me. I kept running until all of a sudden, I went down. I thought I was hit, but I felt no pain. A sniper had hit the belt of my ammo pack, which swung between my legs and tripped me. I sure felt better. But then I looked behind me and saw the next three guys lying face down, all three hit. I got up and ran like hell for the trees and made it.

The next hurdle was the railroad tracks. When enough guys were gathered, we started over. We got hit pretty bad. I got across and threw myself down next to a guy who'd been hit from head to toe by shrapnel on one side. A medic was going through the motions of bandaging him, but he shook his head at me and said, "No way." I lit a cigarette and put it in the guy's mouth. I wished him good luck, but I knew he wasn't going to make it.

We fought our way to a large grove of trees where we thought we had some cover to rest, but the Germans fired artillery into the tops of the trees, which made shrapnel rain straight down on us. They were using phosphorescence shells, which burn right through you if they land on you. That crazy sergeant of ours was singing the song "Buckle Down, Winsocki." That was the first time I ever heard it. Everyone else was trying to find cover, and he was singing.

All of a sudden, the guy next to me started laughing and said, "I got hit in the ass, and I'm out of here." He yelled for a medic, and sure enough, he had a big hole in his ass—the best place to be wounded to get out of the front lines.

Later, we moved out and took the little town of Übach, Germany. At nightfall, we moved out, dug two-men fox holes in a beet field, and waited. At around nine o'clock, we heard German tanks coming toward us with soldiers walking and talking alongside the tanks. They thought we were all in town and that all they had to do was turn the tanks to face the town and blast it with cannon fire and .50 caliber machine guns.

We were standing in our holes to make sure nobody snuck up on us. Next, there was a loud ringing in our ears, and me and my partner saw a big hole between our shoulders. He looked at me and pushed me down.

"You're showing like a light bulb," he said.

The powder from the phosphorous shells was all over me. I rubbed dirt all over myself, but I knew we'd been spotted and had to escape that hole. We crawled on our stomachs for about a hundred yards, then ran into town to the headquarters, where we stayed all night.

The next day, back in my hole, another round hit the edge of it and knocked me whacky. In WWI, this was called shell shock, but so many vets got compensation for shell shock that the Army decided this would not apply in WWII.

[After combat, people often dealt with stuff like ringing in the ears, confusion, memory loss, headaches, dizziness, tremors, and being super sensitive to noise. At the time, they called it Synchondrosis—later changed to Post-Concussion Syndrome (PCS). Now we know it can be a sign of serious PTSD. Back then, it stirred up a ton of controversy. If you didn't have obvious physical injuries, folks just assumed you were weak or lacking in character.]

This meant that if you were so close to a shell burst that you got a concussion, it was your fault. You'd get really, really scared and realize you could have been killed, so if you hadn't thought about it, you would have been okay. Bullshit! I would like to see anyone come that close to death and not be shaking in their boots.

Anyway, I now had Synchondrosis and was sent back to the field hospital in an ambulance that was strafed by a German fighter plane. We were the only vehicle on the road. The driver had to pull in between two buildings to get away from the plane. At the field hospital, a doctor examined and questioned me, and then said I would be returned to a hospital in England for treatment.

I went to hospital in the first town behind the lines. They put me in bed, gave me a blue pill, and knocked me out for six hours. Then they fed me and gave me another blue pill for six more hours of sleep. This was repeated for two days. We later called the pills Blue 88s, after the 88-millimeter German cannons that packed one hell of a punch—just like the pills did.

Finally, they took me to see a doctor. He sat across from me and stared. This made me more nervous than I already was. He asked, "Were you scared?"

"Hell yes," I said. "Everyone on the front line is scared."

Then he looked at the palms of my hands, which were yellow from nicotine stains. I explained that if you smoked in a fox hole, you had to hide the cigarette in your palms so no light showed.

Then he asked, "When was the last time you went to bed, son?"

I thought he'd said "wet the bed," so I answered, "Not since I was a little kid," and he ordered my return to England for treatment.

As I went back to bed, a doctor pulled me and another soldier into a room. He whispered to us that the young soldier, fully conscious and lying in bed, was going to die, and he didn't want him to die alone. We stood by the soldier's bed. He just looked at us, then closed his eyes. It really touched us both, even though we'd already seen so much more violent death.

I was placed on a media ex-paratrooper transport plane to England. Flying over the channel was rough. Everyone got sick except for the medic. When we landed, the pilot stuck his head out of the door and puked; he probably had a hangover.

The first night in hospital, a medic handed out sleeping pills. I said I really didn't need one, and he said okay. Lots of other guys said the same. Ten minutes later, a big fat captain doctor arrived with a huge hypodermic needle and stopped at my bed. "I can't make you take a sleeping pill, but I can make you take this shot." He was trying to scare me, so I said fine and rolled up my sleeve. "Prepare him," he ordered two medics beside him, and they rolled me over and held me down.

He shoved his big needle into the cheek of my butt. It felt like a red-hot poker, but I put a smile on my face and said, "Needles don't bother me." This pissed him off, but all the other guys called out to the medic saying, "I'm ready for my pill now!" Bunch of chickens.

We found out later that the sleeping pill was given because we were starting treatment for shell shock the next day. Nurses and medics came through and gave us each a shot in the morning, turned out the lights, and left. I soon experienced the worst hunger pains, sweating, and weakness I have ever felt. I felt like I was starving to death and was so weak I couldn't lift my arms.

We lay like that for fifteen minutes. Then the lights came on and medical staff rushed in with big glasses of the sweetest orange juice I've ever tasted. They delivered this to everyone and helped them drink it. Then sweet jelly and peanut butter sandwiches were handed out, and we crammed them into our mouths.

Within minutes, we all felt normal. Then they explained—the shots were massive doses of insulin that depleted the sugar in our bodies. After fifteen minutes we would go into shock, so they reversed the effects with loads of sugar. They continued this for five days. We tried to hide food in our beds, but they searched us every morning. We all thought the treatment was a bunch of shit, but there are no shell shock claims out of WWII.

We stayed in the hospital until we were reassigned. One afternoon, Orville walked in. Orville was my brother Duke's best friend, but he was like a brother to all of us Donka kids. Orville was so close to Duke that when Duke died in 1975, Orville married Duke's widow, Mabel.

Orville had gotten word from home that I was there. He worked at an airfield near Kidderminster. I got a pass, and we went out and got drunk. The pub we went to was on a boat anchored on a small lake. When Mom and I visited England in 1987, I drove all around Kidderminster looking for that pub. It was still open. We had a few beers and were welcomed like long-lost friends.

After the so-called treatment, I recovered and went to another repo-depot to await reassignment, which usually took two to three weeks. We were housed in big estate, two or three men to a room. The only thing I remember was getting lost in the fog on the way to breakfast. The mess hall was directly behind our house about a hundred yards, but I roamed around for half an hour until I heard mess kits being rattled and followed the sound. You've never seen fog as thick as in England.

The next camp I was sent to was in Swindon, England. We didn't have much to do, but we got passes almost every night. I liked England very much. The girls were always pretty and sexy. Take them out, buy them some fish and chips, and oh, boy! Of course, a pair of nylons or some cigarettes, or just food from the PX, and you were in like Flynn—except for the land Army girls and their knickers. Of course it didn't bother me because I was only looking for companionship (ahem!).

In general, the English people treated us very well, except for the soldiers and sailors. American soldiers got five times more pay than British soldiers, so we spent a lot more money on girls. In fact, we never walked home alone at night in England because we would have to fight our way home.

As we were about to leave a pub with our dates one night, we saw about six service men eyeing us and knew we were in trouble. We went back in, picked up heavy beer mugs, and returned to the entrance. They came along, saw we were ready and waiting, and said, "Yanks, there won't be a problem."

We could go to pubs, NAFFI clubs, or USO clubs and get food like weenies and beans. At Christmas, there was a book of invitations to spend Christmas in English people's homes. I and another soldier signed up to spend the day with a family. They were on rations but willing to share their food. All the relatives of this family pooled their rations and even served a small roast beef. The PX allowed us to buy canned food and other things that were heavily rationed in England, so we contributed a bit of food and had a great time.

At one time, we were five miles from a bomber airport. We watched them rendezvous over England, and then in formation head to Germany, bomb, and return. The way some of the planes were chopped up, you wondered how they ever made it back to England.

After a few months, I returned to Europe. We were put on a ship with orders. I was to go to Liège, Belgium, to join a truck maintenance outfit, the 344 MAM Co. Our orders gave us free transportation, so my buddy and I caught a train from the coast and headed to Paris.

We decided our orders had no specific time frame, so we sort of partied in Paris. In two days, we were broke. We had our clothes, extra shoes, personal belongings, and everything else we owned in a duffle bag stored in a locker at the train station. Every day, we picked a few pieces of clothing from our locker and sold them in the subway within ten minutes. The French were skilled at making coats out of G.I. blankets.

We made enough daily to cover our expenses. We stayed for a week and probably would still be there if the M.P.s hadn't warned us that if we weren't out of Paris within twenty-four hours, we'd be court-martialed and put in the brig. So we left Paris and headed to Liège. There, I joined the truck maintenance company, but it didn't take them long to discover I had no mechanical skills. Hell, I couldn't even drive.

After two days, the sarge said, "Donka, come with me. I'm going to teach you how to drive."

He picked out a big truck with a covered back, showed me how to shift, and away we went to the site where they ran the repaired trucks through a rough test. We were out there an hour when the sarge said, "Okay, let's head back to our shop."

Now picture this: Our shop was a brick building at the bottom of a very steep hill, about three city blocks long. At the bottom, you turned right through a gate to our shop. There was a guard shack with civilian guards. Now that I knew how to drive, I put it in neutral, thinking I could coast down the hill. I didn't know that rolling downhill fast in neutral would make the truck lose eighty percent brake power.

The sarge was screaming at me, calling me names I knew weren't true, but I couldn't get it back into gear. I just hung on, and at the bottom turned right to go through the gate.

The guard took one look at this truck barreling toward the gate and ran for his dear life. I don't know what everyone was afraid of.

I stopped before I hit the building. We got out, and the sarge was still using bad language. He decided to see what was in the back. That's when he almost fainted. The whole truck was loaded with anti-personal mines. If we had hit anything, they wouldn't have found so much as a fingernail.

For some reason, they wouldn't let me drive anymore. Instead, they sent me and another guy—I wonder how he screwed up?—on a freight train loaded with American military vehicles to France. We had rations and were told to sleep in an ambulance that was on the train and to guard the vehicles.

The trip was under a hundred miles, but the train was sidetracked for all other trains. So we stopped constantly on this short trip. By the third day, we ran out of rations. We were sitting on the side of the train wondering what to do when I spotted some soldiers. I ran over to ask if there was an American base nearby, and they took me to where they were stationed. At the mess hall, I told the sergeant of our predicament. He gave us a good meal and extra rations. He even gave us a nice uncooked roast, about five pounds.

That afternoon, we saw a young French boy near the tracks and called to him. He understood English. We had him bring his parents to us. They hadn't seen a piece of meat like that since before the war. We told them if they cut two small steaks for us and cooked them, they could have the rest of the meat.

They wanted to kiss us. We didn't know if we'd see them again, but a half hour later, they were there: Ma, Pa, brother, sister, the whole family. They brought two plates with steak, salad, fried potatoes, and bread. They were happy, and we got a good meal.

It took five days to reach our destination. When we got there, lo and behold, there wasn't a battery, spare tire, or any removable equipment on any of the twenty trucks. Even my towel hanging on the back of the ambulance was gone. I realized I wasn't a very good train guard.

We caught a passenger train and were back at the truck outfit in two hours. From there, I was moved to some outfit in Antwerp, a port city, and buzz bomb alley number one. We were quartered in a building the Americans called Fegee Flats. Every night at round eight o'clock, Axis Sally, a German radio announcer who spoke English, came on the air. Actually, she was American, but *Home Sweet Home* was her regular Nazi propaganda program aimed at making U.S. forces in Europe feel homesick and demoralized. She was convicted of treason in the U.S. and sentenced to jail. She was in prison from 1949 to 1961.

One night, Sally said, "Hi, all you G.I.s at Fegee Flats! You better write your girlfriends and mothers a letter saying goodbye. We're going to start zeroing in on you with U.1s, U.2s, and buzz bombs."

Now, the U.1 you could hear coming. It sounded like a Ford Model T. When we heard one, we would all say, "Keep going, keep going," because if you could hear it as it passed overhead, you knew you were safe. But if the motor shut off before it was overhead, then the warhead let loose and the trajectory carried it forward. So when we heard it overhead, we knew it couldn't hit us. The U.2 rocket was fast. You couldn't hear it until it hit. U.2 rockets and buzz bombs killed a lot of people.

One evening around five o'clock, I was in the building leaning on a windowsill, reading the *Stars and Stripes* newspaper, when there was one hell of an explosion. It knocked me down, but I wasn't hurt. Soon, people who were hurt and cut up came to our building for aid.

A U.2 rocket had hit about a block away. I don't know how many were killed, but a lot were hurt. That night, Axis Sally came on the radio and said, "Pretty close to all you guys in Fegee Flats. Oh, well, we're getting the range." Lucky for me, I moved out a few days later, but I heard that buzz bombs landed on every side of that building.

I had several interesting jobs after I got back to Europe. For a while, I was a courier and had a special jeep with a bib sign on it that read "Courier." A courier could not be stopped for any reason. At a road block, line of traffic, military or otherwise, I would be waved through. My run was from Liège to ETO headquarters in Brussels. I carried all military papers from outfits stationed in Liège. It was a good job because Brussels was sixty miles away, and once I'd delivered my pouch, I was free.

My boss was a young warrant officer. One day, he told me he had a special job for me the next day and would find a substitute courier to make my run. The next morning, he took me to the Italian POW camp and picked up five POWs, whom we often used for manual labor. They never tried to escape because they were treated well and fed and glad to be out of the war. We took them to a nice brick building. My job was to go through it and pick out the nicest furniture to set up two rooms—one for the colonel and one for my boss. A truck would be back to pick me up at 5 p.m. to return the POWs, and I would have guard duty that night.

By 4:45, I had fixed up the rooms nicely. I told the POWs to rest in the hallway and gave them each a cigarette. I took a walk and heard two girls laughing in a room. I went in and found that they'd been hired as chambermaids. The building was to be the sleeping quarters of officers in the Liège area. The girls were happy to have landed such a nice job.

We got talking and got pretty friendly. All that was in the room was a mattress on the floor. It was pretty close to five when one of the girls slammed the door and locked it. The other girl pushed me onto the mattress, lay down beside me, and said, "We're going to keep you prisoner all night."

Just then, I heard the Army truck blow its horn for me to drive back the POWs. What a predicament! Here were two nice young girls wanting… I don't know what. But I was willing to guess, and I had to go. I did the only honorable (shitty) thing that I could. I said, "Don't say a word and open that door, and I will be back tomorrow, alone." That was the hardest decision I ever had to make.

The next day, I told the warrant officer that I had found some real nice chairs for his and the colonel's rooms and was going back to the house to take them, and that I didn't need any POWs.

"Oh, yeah," he said. "Like hell you are. I saw those two young chambermaids last night, and there's no way you're getting in their pants." He told me that if he caught me within a mile of the building, I'd would go back to Infantry. All my begging and pleading was for naught. Sometimes war really is hell.

I was sent from one outfit to another, and it seems like I never stayed in one place too long. Mainly I was with support groups, truck drivers, and M.P.s. When the war ended, it depended on when your outfit came over as to when you would return to the States. First over, first back home. If you weren't a regular member of the outfit and they were going home, you got transferred to another outfit unless you had the required number of points accrued for time overseas. That's how I got pushed around so much after I got out of the Infantry.

I was in Liège when the war came to an end. All of Europe celebrated for weeks. Dancing in the streets, parades, a lot of loving—it was a happy time.

We didn't really have much work to do, as all of the labor was done by the POWs. Every day, I was put in charge of a number of

POWs and given a task. The German POWs liked to test their supervisors. We carried .45 pistols and carbines. Sometimes the meanest-looking German would walk right up to you to see if you'd draw your pistol or level your carbine. If you did, they wouldn't work for you. They figured you were afraid and would shoot them for any little reason. But if you let them come right up to you without drawing your weapon, they knew you weren't nervous.

One time, when I laid my carbine down to show them how to do something, one of the German POWs picked it up and shoved it back into my hands, saying, "Officer coming." Sure enough, there was an American captain coming toward us. If he had seen my carbine lying there, I probably would have been court-martialed. I gave that POW a cigarette as thanks.

I learned a lot by talking to the POWs who spoke English. They told me there was no reason for them to run away. Most of their cities were in ruins. Where could they go as POWs? They were treated well, fed three meals a day, and would be released as soon as possible. If they ran away, they would be caught and sentenced to prison instead of POW camps. So I always had a good crew, often the same guys, who volunteered for my detail. I always brought tobacco and rolling paper, and at break time I let them smoke. Just an old softie, that's me.

Next, I moved to an outfit in Germany. We took over a German factory that made cranes and lifts. We were billeted to a three-story office building where we didn't have much to do. I guess we were just supposed to be occupying forces. We took over a German beer hall for our club.

On Saturday nights, we'd head to the Quartermaster's to pick up Spam and cheese in an effort to entice the *Fräuleins* to our dances. They could get a bite to eat and some good American whiskey, as we could each buy a quart with our PX rations.

One night, four of my buddies lined up thirteen shot glasses and threw down a $5 bet to see who could finish all thirteen. I started, but I don't remember how far I got because I passed out and was so sick the next day I never got out of bed. Stupid!

There's another story I must tell you. We had German girls working in our kitchen. One was a little fat girl, and every time I came through the chow line, she whispered something to the girl next to her and laugh. I don't know what she said, but I didn't like her. But she was a girlfriend of one of my buddies.

One Saturday night, a friend and I came home drunk. When we saw her at the gate of our camp waiting for her boyfriend, I said to my friend, "She must be hot in the pants, waiting for her boyfriend. You hold her down. I'm going to pack her pants with snow to cool her down."

Boy, did she ever put up a battle. We rolled all over the wet, slushy ground, but I managed to pack a lot of snow where it didn't belong. Sorry about that, but it was all part of my younger days.

It was here that a German who worked for us gave me his Army medals. He was a lieutenant in communications. He told me that his wife had been killed in an American air raid, but he held no animosity toward us. While I was here, we were quarantined for a couple of miserable months for some kind of disease going around.

Finally, it was time for me to return to the U.S. I was going home! They tried to talk us into signing up for three more years with a big bonus, but there wasn't enough money in the world to make me do that.

We shipped to France to catch a boat home. While there, we were offered one souvenir weapon each. Some guys had five or six guns. The men who ran the camps hoped to buy the extra guns up for cheap, but the guys threw them into the latrines instead. I got a Walther pistol, which I gave to Bob when I got home. I arrived home on a Sunday. Everyone was there. We had a big picnic in the yard. So ended my wartime experiences.

Chapter 4: Life After the War

Being home again after twenty-two months in Europe was a great feeling. Seeing towns not damaged from bombs and war was a little bit hard to get used to—just like not being told what to do, when to eat, and all the other sorts of regimentation that you get when you're part of a large army.

After a few weeks, I adjusted and decided it was time to go back to work. So I went back to Stephens & Adams. Bob worked in the steel shop. I worked in the machine shop. Poor Ma, she had a hell of a time getting us up and making our breakfasts and lunches. We were both grouchy and grumbly in the morning, and when she was mad she turned on the radio to a theme song that went, "Get up, get up, smile a while, smile all the whole day through…"

It was about this time I met your mother. I met her at the 129th Club. She was living upstairs at the Guzmans' house. You all know the story. I took one look at her and knew I was sunk. On top of that, she showed me a mosquito bite. I was overcome. She knew she had me in her clutches.

After a summer of heavy romancing, we decided to get married. October 19th, 1946, was the big day. We got married at Helen's house and held the reception at the 129th Club. Ma and the girls cooked all the food. We were having a good time until the pants of my new suit split in the butt. I went home, and Ma sewed it up so I could go back and dance.

We left in a cab about midnight for the Aurora Hotel for our first night together. At that time, it was a nice hotel. The next morning, we took the train into Chicago and spent the day roaming the city. Then I took her to Minsky's Burlesque Show before heading home.

At that time, apartments were very hard to come by, so Ma added a room to her small house (now Bob's front room) for our bedroom and sitting room. We lived there for about a year. It was where Robin was born. Soon after, I quit work at S&A and went to work at Kroehler's Furniture Factory.

We found an upstairs apartment on Baseline Road in Montgomery. It was an old farmhouse with an oil stove for heat. Every two days, I walked a mile to a gasoline station and carried home oil for our stove.

Clarence Balius, Margaret's husband, had a 1942 Ford Roadster that he didn't use, so he gave it to us because we were stranded on this farm. Balius (we never used his first name, he was always just called Balius) really took over as a father to me after my dad died. That's why I always stayed so close to him and Margaret.

Working at Kroehler's, I became a pretty good upholsterer. It wasn't long before I was a team captain, boss of an upholstery line with eleven men on it.

I was there about a year when the workers at Kroehler's went on strike. Around that time, I came home one night to find Sunny and baby Robin in a freezing house. The stove had broken, and the landlord had refused to fix it.

Julia and her husband, Ralph, had an extra bedroom in their home, so I called them. Ralph said, "I'll call Bob and bring the truck and get you out of there tonight." We loaded up the truck with what little furniture we had, tied the dishes and pots and pans into sheets and blankets, threw everything into the back of the truck, and left.

Since Kroehler's was on strike, I took a job with Railroad Express Co. at the Burlington Station on South Broadway in Aurora. We unloaded freight coming to Aurora on passenger trains. It was a good job, and I hoped to work up to seniority, but unfortunately that didn't happen and I was bumped and out of a job again.

At this time, a new bakery called Omar Bakery, which delivered door to door, had opened up in Aurora. I applied and got the territory of Glen Ellyn. A supervisor accompanied me the first week. We went door to door selling bread, cakes, cookies, and so on, and enlisted customers for new orders. We would deliver one day and get orders for deliveries every second day.

I did this for about three months, going to the bakery at five a.m. to load up, then heading out to Glen Ellyn. I had to pay the bakery cash for what I sold, except for the customers that had charge accounts, and I had to supply my own change—but I was always coming up short!

I wouldn't get home until 6:30 in the evening, so Robin was asleep when I left and asleep when I returned. I didn't get to spend much time with him except on Sundays. I had run myself ragged and lost twenty pounds. Dr. Morris, our family doctor, said I needed to quit that job.

The only job I could find was at Gordon's Junkyard. I worked with John Sabo, sorting the good junk—brass, copper, and the like—from the bad. I worked there for about two weeks until Gordon fired me. It was the only time I was ever fired, and it was from a junkyard.

That reminds me when we were kids and collected junk, Izzy Gordon would always buy it from us. He knew we were poor and he never cheated us. Sometimes he would let us go through his paper pile and take out the funny books—*Flash Gordon*, *Batman*, *Terry and the Pirates*, *Tarzan*, *Robin Hood*. When we were through with them, we took a big bag and sold it back to him. He knew they were the books he'd given us, but he still give us a nickel or a dime. He had a good heart.

Finally, the strike at Kroehler's ended and I went back to work for them. I was called to the plant manager's office one day. He instructed me to go out and buy any books on management that I could find and said he'd pay for them. He told me to read them and to come back and see him when I had.

It took me about two months to read those dull books, but I did. I made an appointment to go to his office and see him. He sat me down and gave me a two-hour test, then said he'd let me know the results.

A week later, he informed me that I had scored at the collegiate level on the test—me, with three years of high school who never got above a C. I was so surprised! He said that they'd been watching my progress as a team captain and wanted to start moving me up the ladder, first as a foreman, then superintendent, and so forth.

At the time, I was making ten percent over what my line made. My foreman made ten percent over me, but he worked eight hours more at no extra pay. The superintendent made a little more but was on a fixed salary and worked long, long hours. I pointed this out, but he mentioned how prestigious it would be to be higher up in the company.

I said, "The time is not worth it," and he said, "Goodbye, young man," and showed me to the door. So much for prestige.

A foreman who had worked at Kroehler's, Paul Yaeger, quit and joined the Pullman Furniture Co. in Chicago as a supervisor. He convinced the company that he could bring ten key men from Kroehler's with the knowledge to set up upholstery lines using their methods, which would bring a big profit for their company.

They grabbed at the chance. So ten of us were promised $2.50 an hour, with the understanding that we would be made foremen once we established our methods.

I could reweave flaws in material and save lots of money. If the flaws weren't caught until flaw inspections, it saved tearing the furniture apart to replace the fabric. I could reweave it and you could never see the flaw. I was pretty good at this.

We started our own upholstery line using these methods, which would now be considered industrial espionage—using another company's methods.

The Pullman Co. was large, employing many more people than Kroehler. About three quarters of the workers were Black. They treated us well until they found out why we were there. Their methods were a lot slower than ours. They could bring quarts of beer to work as long as they kept them in bags, and they liked this laid back way of working.

The foreman and supervisor saw how they might lose their jobs, so they got together and started giving us bad material to work on—frames made wrongly, covers not big enough to work with, or anything they thought would make us look bad.

We knew we were in trouble when they started hassling us and calling us down. We took it for a week until one day, it got real bad. We thought we wouldn't get out without being badly injured, so we picked up our upholstery scissors—about twelve inches long—to protect ourselves.

It got pretty nasty until one young Black guy came up and said,

117

"We have nothing personal against you. We just don't like the way you work."

That was when I decided it was time for me to move on and get work closer to home.

Ernie's Story: Afterword

This is where Dad ended his story. My feeling is his health and cancer had made a turn for the worse and he never got to finish his telling his tale. So I will fill in a few details.

Dad died on May 11, 2002, after a long battle with cancer. In the days before he passed, he spoke of seeing his ma and other family members out his hospital window. They were telling him to come on over, they were ready for him. My sister and I encouraged him to join them. We had all been there throughout the week—his children and grandchildren, Mom, and his remaining brothers and sisters.

At moments, Dad was alert and funny. He asked his grandson Aaron if he knew how to drive. When Aaron said yes, Dad replied, "Then drive this bed out of here!"

In 1956, Dad joined the Aurora Fire Department, where he worked his way up to captain and then retired in 1978. In 1971, he was honored as fireman of the year for saving a child from a burning building. In 1977, he bought a small fire protection business that employed a few off-duty and retired firefighters. My brother Dave joined the company and grew it to a very successful business.

He always had part-time jobs, as the working at the fire department was one twenty-four hour shift on and then forty-eight hours off. For many years, he worked part time at the local furniture store. He also cleaned several different doctors' offices in Aurora in the evenings. I would often go with him and do the dusting, and he would pay me five dollars for my help.

With four children to raise, he and Mom both worked. Mom and Aunt Virginia worked part time for a catering company, and I often went to work with them and helped bus tables. Mom also worked for a time at a local public school as a kindergarten teacher's assistant. She collected old clothing from people and took it to the poor children who often came to school without coats and gloves and hats in the winter. Mom also worked for an eye doctor for many years until finally going to work for Aurora Pump as a secretary, where she worked until she retired.

Ernie and Sunny—no one ever called her Mary, since Dad's mother and one of his sisters were also named Mary. Mom told everyone to call her Sunny, the nickname given to her by a Canadian pilot—went on to raise four children right next door to the house Dad grew up in, and across the street from where Mom first lived with Gail, on Indian Avenue. The Donka clan all lived close by. Uncle Bob raised his family on Dearborn Avenue in the house that Grandma moved to after Grandpa died. Grandma lived there with Bob and his family until her death in 1965.

Next door to Bob were Loui and Mabel, and next door to them were Mary and Clarence. Across the street were Julia and Ralph. On our street, four doors down from us, were Frank and Marie. Behind them were Helen and Tubby. Anna and Whitey lived a few blocks away, just over the Dearborn Avenue bridge, and Margaret and Clarence lived right behind the ball park. Uncle Dave and Aunt Rita were the only ones not in walking distance. They lived on the west side of Aurora.

The Donka clan stuck together through thick and thin. I don't think it was always easy for Mom, a divorced British war bride brought up completely different from the crazy Hungarians. But the sisters-in-law—Virginia, Marie, Rita, and Mabel—all stuck together and helped Mom find her place and voice within the Donka clan. The Donkas continued to have family summer picnics all throughout my childhood, every Memorial Day, Fourth of July, and Labor Day.

We grew up with family all around us. On summer evenings, we often gathered at Uncle Bob's with the aunts and uncles and cousins. When Grandma was alive, you had to walk up to where she was sitting on the porch and give her a kiss on the cheek. She didn't speak much English, so there was not a lot of talking.

The grownups drank beer while the kids ran through the connected yards playing games and collecting fireflies. There was always laughter and arguments and love. Every Christmas, we had a tradition we called "making the rounds." We started at around five in the evening at one house, often Uncle Bob's while Grandma was alive, for a cocktail and appetizers. Then we walked to the other three nearby houses and had more cocktails and more food. We continued on, driving to all the other aunts and uncles, doing the same thing. At the last house, we had a supper of stuffed cabbages and ham. Sometimes, if Dad was sober enough, we attended midnight Mass. I don't remember a Christmas when we didn't participate in this tradition.

Ernie and Sunny had four children, and as of today, they have eight grandchildren and ten great-grandchildren. Their life together was good. My dad adored my mom, and he gave her the love, security, and family she had always longed for. I think my mom always wondered about her past and who her birth parents were, but she mostly put it aside and lived her life fully.

Later in her life, I realized she probably suffered from depression, as there were times throughout my childhood—and more often in her later years—when she erupted with anger for some unseeable reason. As I got older, I recognized the pattern of her going down that dark hole, then the explosion of anger, and then it would pass and she would be fine for months. Dad always dealt with her with kindness and compassion. That was just who he was.

When Dad died in 2002, it was very hard on Mom. She once again felt abandoned and alone, but she really did remarkably well. She "pulled herself up by her boots straps," a saying she always used, and went on to have a full and happy life for the next eighteen years.

She traveled all over with a group of folks from her bank, of all places. I joined them once on a trip to England and Scotland for her eighty-fifth birthday. She also took a trip with the bank to Alaska and a few other places. In her late eighties, she decided to come live by me in Gunnison, Colorado. She bought a condo, volunteered at our local museum, and joined an exercise class at our local recreational center. This place also offered senior lunches, and she made many friends there.

She said she would never marry again and was not interested in any sort of relationship other than friendship. Sometime after her ninetieth birthday, she decided she wanted to move back home to be near my sister, Cindy, and her grandchildren, who lived in Wisconsin. Mom lived in a retirement community until signs of dementia started to appear and it became obvious that living alone was no longer an option.

We found a nice private facility for her to live in just minutes from Cindy's house. But Mom was not happy there, and after about six months, she made that very clear, so Cindy took her home.

Thinking back on it now, she probably didn't want to die in an institution of any sort. I'm sure those early memories of being in the orphanage were buried somewhere deep inside of her, and she wasn't having it. So Cindy, who thankfully had nursing skills, took care of Mom for the last year and a half of her life with grace, kindness, and humor, which was greatly needed. I am so grateful, as this was during Covid. Had Mom still been in the home, we wouldn't have been able to be with her, and she would have probably died all alone. This would have been horrible for all of us.

The last three weeks of Mom's life were filled with lots of love from her family. My brother Dave and his family came up on the weekends to see her, and it was a beautiful time. Mom talked about going home and seeing Dad and her parents, and she told us how much she loved us. A priest came and gave her the Last Rites, which I think was important to her.

She was surrounded by her family when she left this world to join my dad and brother, Robin, who died in 2017, and to learn the answers to the questions of her true life story.

Afterword

by Candace Carson

When I first started this project of transcribing my parents' memoirs, I originally planned on just doing it for my family members—but as I delved further into their stories, I began to realize that they were giving us a real snapshot of a time in history that all of us can learn from. So I decided I wanted to share their experiences with the world.

Their stories described many small details of what life was like in the 1930s and 1940s in the United States and England. I, like many people, love to watch *The Glided Age* and *Downton Abbey*, as they are pieces of history that fascinate us, but they mostly portray the wealthy people of that time.

My parents' stories are more like Frank McCourts book *Angela's Ashes* or John Irving's *The Cider House Rules*. These stories describe life of the working class and of the poor, which are my parents' stories.

As we find ourselves in this particular time history, where we are in such flux and uncertainty, I think it's good to remember how far we have come and to ask ourselves: Do we want to repeat the history of division and hate?

We glamorize the glided age, but for the working poor, there was a lot of suffering and hardship.

My father was a lighthearted and funny man, and he took life as it came to him. As he says in his memoir, "We were poor but happy."

Mom's favorite sayings was, "Just pull yourself up from your bootstraps," which is what she did most of her life.

We can learn from their experiences, and we can learn from the past. I am grateful for the large extended family I grew up with, and I am grateful for the love that I was given.

Acknowledgments

Special thanks to my friend Enid Holden for her editing assistance, and to my amazing publisher, Vince Font—I could not have finished this book without him. His patience, kindness, and insight was more than I could have ever expected. He made the whole process easy and fun. You are the best!

I would also like to express my sincerest gratitude to my niece Alex Carey and my cousin Charlotte Underwood for all of their work and searching to find and connect our families. Without your dedication and curiosity, none of this would have been possible. To my cousin June Donka, thank you for all of your research on the Donka family, for guiding me through Ancestry, and supporting my journey with love and humor. To my siblings David and Cindy, I am so grateful that we have always had each other to lean on, through thick and thin. I am blessed to have you in my life. I know that somewhere, my brother Robin is cheering me on as he always did. Without him, I would not be where I am today. And last but not least, my loving husband, Dan, always there supporting me in my next adventure. Thank you for loving me and always taking care of me.

About the Author

Candace Carson is also the author of *Diary Of A Deadhead: A Wild Magical Ride into the World of Sound and Vibration* (2015). Find the book in digital and paperback format on Amazon, Barnes & Noble, and elsewhere.

About the Publisher

Glass Spider Publishing is a hybrid publisher made up of a small team of professional writers, editors, artists, and designers with a shared passion for storytelling. The company was founded in 2016 by award-winning author Vince Font to help bring the work of underrepresented writers to light. For more information, visit www.glassspiderpublishing.com.

www.ingramcontent.com/pod-product-compliance
Lightning Source LLC
Chambersburg PA
CBHW021117130626
46554CB00002B/735